Zeal for Thy House

Suffering Through Mass

By

Jay Boyd, Ph.D.

Acknowledgements

I must first acknowledge and thank my husband, Jerry Boyd, who has encouraged me in my "career" as a blogger and writer. His patience for my passion seems endless, and he never complains about the housework that hasn't been done.

I also thank Terry Carroll, Executive Producer at ChurchMilitant.TV. He is a good friend, an inspiration, and a contributor to my blog and my books. And I still have not met him face-to-face!

The person who has influenced me the most with regard to my knowledge and perceptions of "good liturgy" will remain nameless here, but I'll tell you about the path upon which he has guided me.

From my first interactions with him, I found him to be full of knowledge about the Church, and his love and reverence for liturgy were readily apparent. He patiently listened to and answered all of my questions about the Church. He seldom answered me from his own opinion, though; his answers always included references to Church documents. He has taught me where to find the sources, and often provides me with some history on the more important encyclicals and instructions.

Through his guidance, I came to a greater understanding of and reverence for the Mass – through his own love of it, and his faithful adherence to the rubrics. Before his ordination, when he was limited to celebrating the Liturgy of the Pre-Sanctified Gifts, the communion services he led were more reverent than any Mass I'd ever attended. When I commented on this, he introduced me to the *General Instruction of the Roman Missal* (*GIRM*) and *Redemptionis Sacramentum.* Being a student at heart, I embraced the teaching and the documents, and he led me to more and more of the rich treasury of writings on the Liturgy. It's been a mixed blessing, though, as I have become more aware of the abuses, small and large. It's been a heart-breaking and painful journey.

It is difficult to put into words the impact this priest has had on me – on my love for the Church, on my appreciation of her liturgies, and on my prayer life. I pray his devotion to the Mass and his fidelity to the Church will impact our entire diocese.

About the Author

I was born in Rochester, New York, and reared mostly in Concord, California. I was a very good student in high school, but spent a good deal of time "finding myself" in my college years. Still, I ended up completing a two-year degree in Forestry Technology, followed a lifetime later by a Bachelor of Arts in Psychology. I earned a doctorate in Developmental Psychology at the University of California, Santa Barbara, in 1989, and taught a few years at the college level. So much for my education…

After a long and shady history, I, a baptized-but-fallen-away-Episcopalian-turned-born-again-Christian, ended up marrying Jerry, a cradle Catholic. I went to Mass with him regularly at first, but attended services at my Pentecostal church as well. Eventually, I grew weary of the Catholic Mass, and just stuck with my Pentecostal Sunday services. On Sundays, then, Jerry and I went our separate ways. This went on for a number of years.

Eventually, though, the Holy Spirit managed to impress upon my mind and heart the Truth of the Real Presence of Jesus in the Eucharist. Once I understood that, I couldn't wait to become Catholic. I was received into the Catholic Church in 2002, contrary to all expectations of my husband.

Since my conversion, I've invested quite a lot of time and energy into understanding and proclaiming the authentic teaching of the Magisterium, especially with regard to life issues and the sacred liturgy. Over the years, I gathered my thoughts and wrote a few articles on these topics, published in *Homiletic and Pastoral Review*.

My life's work, though, has involved pouring my time and energy, heart and soul, into the rearing of two children who have grown up to be a couple of the most wonderful people you'd ever want to meet. I freely admit, of course, that this has much more to do with God's grace than my own abilities as a mother.

I blog at "Philothea On Phire"[1]. I chose that blog title because of my fondness for St. Francis de Sales, patron saint of Catholic writers, as well as the patron saint of the parish and diocese in which I reside. "You aim at a devout life, dear Philothea, because as a Christian you know that such devotion is most acceptable to God's Divine Majesty," says the Saint in his book *Introduction to the Devout Life*. "I have made use of a name suitable to all who seek the devout life, Philothea meaning one who loves God."

---

[1] http://philotheaonphire.blogspot.com

O Most Holy Trinity,
Father, Son, and Holy Ghost,
I offer to You
the most Precious Body and Blood,
Soul and Divinity of Jesus Christ,
present in all the tabernacles of the world,
in reparation for the sacrileges,
outrages, and indifference
by which He Himself is offended.

And through the infinite merits
of His most Sacred Heart
and the Immaculate Heart of Mary,
I beg of you the conversion of poor sinners.

Table of Contents

Introductory Remarks

Section I: Liturgical Abuse

Section II: The *Novus Ordo*

Section III: The Music at Mass

Section IV: The Extraordinary Form of the Mass

Section V: Dealing With It

Epilogue

Appendices

Preface

I was received into the Catholic Church in 2002. As I have written elsewhere[2]:

> My journey into Catholicism included teaching religion classes at a Catholic high school during my RCIA year, including serving as the "Campus Ministry" instructor; I was responsible for leading a class in "creating" the liturgy for a monthly "first Friday Mass" for the school. I was not even Catholic at the time, and really had no inkling as to how to proceed with the liturgy; I asked if there were a manual of some sort. "Oh no," I was told. "Just ask the kids. They know how to do it. They'll teach you." Again, hindsight reveals that one important treasure had been hidden from me even when I asked for it: the *General Instruction of the Roman Missal.*

Later, I learned about the existence of the *GIRM*, and, being a student at heart, I studied it. My spiritual director pointed me to many other documents and books on the subject of the Liturgy, and I read and studied those as well. And being a good student, I did what students are usually required to do in a class: I wrote papers. A few of those papers have been published in *Homiletic and Pastoral Review*, and two of them appear in this book.

I was excited about what I was learning, and since I worked as the parish secretary, it was easy to offer my new knowledge for the sake of improving the liturgical practices that I observed weekly at Mass. Unfortunately, my efforts went unrewarded…to say the least. And I discovered over the course of the next few years that many others who, like me, desired and asked for sound liturgy that follows the rubrics and lifts our minds and hearts to God, had met with the same

---

[2] See the Introduction: "We've Been Robbed", p. xx;

reluctance – and even animosity – that I encountered. "We've always done it this way," was the oft-heard refrain, and no one wanted to do it "right". After all, "do you think God really cares about that?" Well, yes, I *do* think that. I believe He cares very much. That's why I decided that certain things needed to be said, whether or not anyone paid any attention.

And because I believe God cares "about that", I am passionate about the liturgy, and I am passionate about the truth. Out of that passion, I started writing about my frustration with liturgical abuse and the general irreverence I witnessed at Mass, trying to present a reasoned and logical approach to *why* God cares and why we should try to follow the mind of the Church where liturgy is concerned. In September of 2011, I created a blog which I dubbed "Philothea on Phire"[3]. I freely admit that my main purpose for the blog was to vent; I told my spiritual director that I felt that there were things that needed to be said, and that I wanted to say them, even if no one else listened. My primary concern was the Mass.

I like things to be laid out clearly. I'm not always good at doing that myself, of course; and sometimes I'm *too* good at it, which is generally called "lacking in tact" or being "uncharitable". Some think it's "calling a spade a spade". Once, I asked my spiritual director how I should introduce myself to a priest I was planning to visit. He suggested, "The indefatigable blog-mistress of Philothea-on-Phire, terror of bishops and errant clergy". I like that better than "nit-picking, nattering nabob", which one commenter suggested.

Through my blog, I not only found a way to voice my frustrations in a public forum, I found like-minded souls who enjoyed reading what I wrote. The phrase "misery loves company" comes to mind! At any rate, I hope that, together, we can encourage and support each other in our efforts to bring good liturgy to our respective parishes, and thereby do some good for the universal Church.

Introduction

The main purpose of this book is twofold, though the purposes might seem at first to be a bit at odds with each other.

The first purpose is to expose some problems in the Church today – in particular, the problem of liturgical abuses, and the problem of the reluctance of many parishes to provide the extraordinary form of the Mass for those who desire it. The second purpose is to show that, despite these problems, there is a glimmer of hope – and we should never, ever give up hope!

I have other aspirations for this book, too, though. I hope that those who experience pain and suffering at the Masses offered at their parishes will find some solace in knowing that they are not the only ones! It is helpful to recognize that we are not alone in the battle to have liturgies properly celebrated. I hope also to show in these pages that the pain and suffering is *real*, and that it is justified by the fact that the Church has shown us clearly how the Mass – whether the old form or the new form – should be celebrated. We are not wrong or "divisive" if we voice objections and concern when the rubrics of the Mass are ignored or altered to suit the personality of the celebrant or, in some cases, the "liturgy committee". Whether the abuses and missteps are intentional or made through ignorance, the pain and suffering of those who desire good liturgy is legitimate, and deserves to be heeded.

Requesting a properly celebrated Mass is a right that we have as lay faithful, and that right is examined in these pages (see in particular the chapters entitled "A Liturgical Bill of Rights", p. 27, and "Liturgical Rights and Liturgical Rites", p. 33). The rubrics are there for a reason; the Church does not capriciously demand adherence to

---

[3] http://philotheaonphire.blogspot.com

insignificant details! There are consequences of liturgical abuse. In a homily addressing those consequences, an anonymous priest said the following (my **emphases**):

It is fair to say that the liturgy **directly forms** our notion of the holiness of God. Look at Sinai. Look at the tabernacle. Look at the sanctuary. God has designed the structure of reality in such a way that the liturgy repairs and restores Creation. It re-establishes the limits and restores the damages unleashed by sin.

What goes on in the Divine Liturgy determines what goes on out in the world. The graces that were lost by Adam, the terrible offences that have been offered to God, the liturgy makes amends for this. The liturgy reorders our fallen world. And once we realize that the **liturgy reorders all of creation**, we can begin to understand the **horror of liturgical abu**se. What is a priest saying when he deliberately abuses the liturgy?

Symbolically, liturgically, he is re-enacting the Original Sin right in God's face. Instead of order, he is bringing disorder; instead of grace, he's bringing sin; instead of spiritual health, he's bringing spiritual sickness; instead of everlasting life, he's bringing spiritual death. Instead of keeping the serpents out of the garden and away from his people, he's turning to them and inviting them to come on in. In effect, the priest is saying, "I will not serve; I'll do it my way. I will dictate liturgical relationships to God. I will set myself apart from His Law. I will be a law unto myself. I will exalt myself". He's imitating the sons of Aaron, and unless he repents, he'll get the same kind of punishment.

But it isn't just the priest who's going to suffer, **we're all going to suffer**. All of us. What goes on in the Divine

Liturgy determines what goes on in the world – that's reality. That's the way it is. So what're we saying? We're saying that when massive numbers of the officially appointed ambassadors who represent the Church Militant before the Divine Court, when massive amounts of these divinely appointed ambassadors – that is to say priests – are constantly and consistently re-enacting Original Sin right in the face of God, we're gonna get exactly what we got the first time: sin, suffering, nakedness, disorder, despair, death, and the reign of Satan.

We're saying we're going to get exactly what we are getting: this culture of death, this present darkness, this new paganism. **The culture of death is the natural result of massive liturgical abuse.** [I repeat: the] *culture of death is the natural result of massive liturgical abuse.* The most important aspect of the solution to the problem – of all these kinds of societal problems – is liturgical. It always has been, and it always will be. St. Alphonsus says,

> The Lord commanded the priests of the Old Law to tremble, to reverence, when approaching the sanctuary, and still we see scandalous irreverence in priests in the New Law when they stand at the altar in the presence of Jesus Christ.

St. Teresa of Avila used to say,

> I would give my life for a ceremony of the Church and will a priest despise the ceremonies of the Holy Mass?[4]

---

[4] *This is an excerpt from a homily entitled "The Importance of the Liturgy in the Holy Sacrifice of the Mass"; an audio recording is available at http://www.audiosancto.org/sermon/20061112-The-Importance-of-the-Liturgy-in-the-Holy-Sacrifice-of-the-Mass.html. The written excerpt itself also appears at the link.*

Indeed, there *are* consequences of liturgical abuse, and those who recognize abuses have a duty to seek the rectification of those abuses. For those who suffer through Mass and who wish to help their pastors restore awe and reverence to their liturgical practices, I hope this book will provide the documentation need to help them understand their own pain and to help them explain to those who will listen *why* good liturgy is important...and that "good liturgy" is defined by the Church, not by our own personal "feelings" about the way Mass is celebrated.

As I mentioned above, I also want to encourage those who suffer through Mass to cling to the hope that brighter liturgical days are ahead. To that end, I have included at the end of each section a few "Glimmers of Hope". All is not lost! The gates of Hell will not prevail! Hope springs eternal!

"We've Been Robbed!"

This article was published in Homiletic and Pastoral Review, May 2008. HPR is now a web-only publication at www.hprweb.com.

It was Easter Vigil, 2002. I was being received into the Catholic Church. I had been robbed, and I didn't even know it.

Perhaps "robbed" isn't the correct word, but in hindsight, I can see clearly that some of the most wonderful treasures of the Roman Catholic Church had at least been hidden from my view. At the time, however, I didn't even know they existed.

The real sense that I had been robbed has come only recently for me, and the catalyst has been the Holy Father's *motu proprio, Summorum Pontificum.*

Having not been Catholic prior to Vatican II, nor even for much of the post-Vatican II era, I had no knowledge of the traditional Latin Mass, the *forma extraordinaria.* I'd had no exposure to Latin until a year or so after I'd been received into the Church, but when I had received that exposure to the official language of the Church, I was "sold" – another treasure had been "discovered"! I started teaching myself Latin, and began memorizing some of the traditional prayers in Latin. When the *Compendium* of the *Catechism of the Catholic Church* was published, I was delighted to discover a whole section of prayers in English *and* Latin.

Finally, I have now experienced the extraordinary form of the Mass: a treasure, it seems to me, of inestimable value. And now I find myself crying out, "We were robbed!"

What, exactly, was taken? Let me backtrack a bit, and give my impressions as a convert to the faith who has no formal training in these matters.

I'd educated myself prior to attending RCIA classes by reading through parts of the *Catechism of the Catholic Church.* I'd originally purchased my own volume in order to read it and find ways to prove to my cradle-Catholic husband that the Catholic Church was *wrong* with regard to a variety of issues. In fact, I found what appeared to me to be beautiful, sound doctrine, and I could not find anything "wrong" with it. Here was a treasure which had not been hidden! I did wonder, however, why the wonderful teaching in that book did not seem to be very adequately implemented in every-day practice. Apparently, the treasure had been hidden from many Catholics – or else they had chosen to ignore it.

My journey into Catholicism included teaching religion classes at a Catholic high school during my RCIA year, including serving as the "Campus Ministry" instructor; I was responsible for leading a class in "creating" the liturgy for a monthly "first Friday Mass" for the school. I was not even Catholic at the time, and really had no inkling as to how to proceed with the liturgy; I asked if there were a manual of some sort. "Oh no," I was told. "Just ask the kids. They know how to do it. They'll teach you." Again, hindsight reveals that one important treasure had been hidden from me even when I asked for it: the *General Instruction of the Roman Missal.*

Just before my first anniversary as a Catholic, we moved to a new state and a new parish. In no time at all, I found myself employed as the parish secretary. This provided me with new insights into the "inner workings" of the Church at the parish level, revealing more division than I cared to know about: a deacon, Director of Religious Education, and extraordinary ministers who all questioned Church teaching on such important issues as artificial contraception, homosexuality, and even abortion! We were led by a pastor who was fond of saying (rather ungrammatically) that we needed to "meet people where they're at". He made no mention of moving them along the road to sanctification. In fact, much debate was stirred by our bishop's publication of a pastoral letter prescribing greater fidelity to the *GIRM,* with a vocal minority of parishioners accusing him of being "pre-Vatican II". This prompted me to read the Vatican II documents in order to find out for myself what Vatican II was all about. In the process, I discovered that more treasures had been obscured.

Soon I was introduced to other documents of the Church, and, being a student at heart, I began reading them. Yes, here were even more treasures – a vast storehouse of them!

My "discovery" of the *GIRM* and other documents of the Church, and the realization that these were treasures, did not immediately lead me to the impression that I had been "robbed". To me it seemed that I simply had been unaware of them, though I wondered why they seemed to be the best kept secret of the Catholic Church next to the Real Presence of Jesus in the Eucharist! I saw that they were treasures because they did not "restrict" our liturgical worship, but rather enhanced it by guiding us to greater reverence and appreciation of the mysteries of our faith; they did not "restrict" our morality, but rather provided knowledge that could liberate us from our sin.

The present situation in my parish is not much different from that in many parishes, I suspect: before Sunday Mass begins, the Rosary is prayed. This is wonderful. Then there follows something of a "social" time, which seems to me to detract from the preparation for the Mass that the Rosary has just afforded us. People in the pews chat for a few minutes before the announcer stands before the microphone and bids us "good morning" and other platitudes meant to welcome us and make us feel good. We are invited to "take a moment of silence to prepare out hearts and minds for the Holy Sacrifice of the Mass" (although a few announcers cannot bring themselves to say "holy sacrifice" and deviate from the script by substituting "celebration"). After 30 seconds or so, the "opening hymn" is announced, and Mass has officially started.

This is in stark contrast to the start of Mass in the *forma extraordinaria*. The *Asperges* seems to me to be a wonderful preparation. It reminds us of our sinfulness and of God's mercy in cleansing us of that sin. In fact, throughout the prayers of the Mass of the extraordinary form, I find this constant reminder of the tension between our sin and the mercy of the Father. Not only this, but the penitential rite of the *forma extraordinaria* continues this examination of conscience and petition for forgiveness in a more intense way than occurs in the *Novus Ordo*, or *forma ordinaria*.

Of course, the *Novus Ordo* also offers an opportunity to examine and confess our sins in a meaningful way. The problem is that liturgical abuses have so marred the ordinary form that the differences between it and the extraordinary form are exacerbated. The fault lies not in the *Novus Ordo* itself, but rather in its implementation, in the flagrant disregard for the norms set forth in the *GIRM*.

Returning to some of the differences between the two forms, let us examine, for example, the offertory prayer. From the *forma ordinaria*, we hear "Blessed are you, Lord God of all Creation; through your goodness we have this bread to offer, which earth has given and human hands have made. It will become for us the bread of life."

But in the *forma extraordinaria*, we find a much richer prayer: "Accept, O Holy Father, Almighty and Everlasting God, this unspotted Host, which I, Thine unworthy servant, offer unto Thee, my living and true God, to atone for my countless sins, offenses, and negligences: on behalf of all here present and likewise for all faithful Christians, living and dead, that it may avail both me and them as a means of salvation, unto life everlasting."

To me, the difference between the two prayers is like the difference between sending a text message on a cell phone, and having an actual face-to-face conversation with the Person. Have we reduced ourselves to prayers of the form "Tnx. Pls bless r gifts"?

The difference between the prayers points to something greater than the spoken (or silent) words for me. For one thing, the prayer of the 1962 missal seems to imply a much greater God than the newer prayer. Also, our sins are acknowledged and forgiveness asked within the context of the offertory. And finally, the older prayer underscores the role of the priest: the very words tell us that he is making the offering on our behalf, and acknowledging our sins as well as his own, and asking for us and for himself "life everlasting".

This issue of the role of the priest is an important one, and, to my way of thinking, it constitutes a major difference between the two forms of the Mass. This was an issue I pondered before I knew about the *forma extraordinaria*: the priest as *priest* versus the priest as narrator and commentator.

From my perspective as a new Catholic coming from a Pentecostal Protestant experience, the idea of a priest celebrating Mass facing the people seemed normal, acceptable, and even to be expected. In addition, coming from a tradition where preaching was of the utmost importance (and went on for a long period of time!), having a priest deliver a homily that he tried to make "interesting" to the people also seemed natural. However, as time went on, and I read more about the Mass, including studying the *GIRM*, and reading books on the liturgy (such as *The Spirit of the Liturgy*, both the version by Romano Guardini and the one by then-Cardinal Ratzinger; and *Turning Towards the Lord*, by U.W. Lang), I began to see the problems inherent in having the priest facing the people. The priests of my limited experience seemed to feel that they must take the role of a talk-show host: they adlibbed prayers and encouraged actions by the congregation which were either not prescribed in the rubrics, or explicitly forbidden! In other words, the priest had become the *master* of the Sacred Liturgy rather than its servant.

In the *forma extraordinaria*, it seems that the priest is allowed to be a *priest*, defined as one who offers the prayers of the people to God. The *Catechism* states:

> The ministerial priesthood has the task not only of representing Christ – Head of the Church – before the assembly of the faithful, but also of acting in the name of the whole Church when presenting to God the prayer of the Church, and above all when offering the Eucharistic sacrifice. (§1552).

This is quite evident in the extraordinary form. The priest turns to God, facing *in the same direction* as the people, leading them. He prays most of the prayers without requiring their audible participation, because he is taking the prayers to God *for* us. The altar servers make response for us, though we may join in. Is there still "active participation" by the laity? Certainly: any prayer, whether it is audible or not, reflects "participation"! In fact, prayerful participation is sometimes facilitated by the fact that the laity does not have to take a priestly role, and by the natural silences that occur within the liturgy. The hierarchy of the Church is clearly evident in the extraordinary form, and the role each participant plays is quite clear. There is no clericalization of the laity, and no laicization of the clergy.

Again, it should be noted that the *forma ordinaria* does not require a priest to appear as a talk-show host! The *forma ordinaria* may certainly be celebrated *ad orientem* – with the priest facing the same direction as the people; in fact, certain sections of the *GIRM* assume that he is doing so (e.g., the instruction says something similar to "facing the people, the priest says…" If he were already facing the people, such instruction would be unnecessary). The *forma ordinaria* may be, and certainly is, in some places, celebrated without abuse and with great reverence and devotion by priests who follow the rubrics. In fact, one of the anticipated benefits of the liberalization of the *forma extraordinaria* is that it will lead to greater adherence to the rubrics in the *forma ordinaria* – the "gravitational pull" that has been discussed on various blogs and by various authors.

I recently viewed a DVD of the September 14th Mass in the extraordinary form televised by EWTN. Observing this Mass with most of the levels of the hierarchy represented (lacking a bishop), I was struck by the clear presentation of that hierarchy. Only priests approached the altar. The steps leading up to the altar were utilized to show that one office was "above" another. The subdeacon served the deacon. The deacon served the priest. No lay person entered the sanctuary. The men serving in different ministerial roles vested appropriate to the ministry (e.g., even though the subdeacon was in fact an ordained priest, he vested as a subdeacon).

And all of this reverent attention to detail and hierarchy only served to underscore the Presence of the One who is above all: Our Lord Jesus Christ, King of Kings, Lord of Lords, God of the Universe.

I was in awe as I watched the video. I saw how much is *lacking* in the way many parishes celebrate the *forma ordinaria*. I understood why the alleged percentage of Catholics who actually believe in the Real Presence of Jesus in the Eucharist is so alarmingly low. The *forma extraordinaria* leaves no doubt as to His Real Presence, while the behavior of many of the ministers in the *forma ordinaria* Masses I have attended has often suggested that they are oblivious to Him.

I became very, very much aware of the fact that *we have been robbed.*

I have acquired a copy of the Baronius Press daily missal of 1962 (reprinted in 2004). Included in its title are the words "liturgical manual" – and so it is. It includes a section called "The most necessary Prayers". I found the wording quaint, but what immediately struck me was the difference in attitude such a title suggests in comparison to today's attitude toward formal prayers. Today, I joked to a friend, we would not say "the most necessary prayers" for fear of offending someone whose favorite devotion was not included. We would be afraid to judge some prayers more "necessary" than others. We would not want to suggest that there are *any* "necessary" prayers; instead, we would say, "Here are some prayers that you might want to pray…if you feel like it…once in awhile, anyway…but we're not trying to say that you *should* pray these prayers…if there are some others that you prefer…"

Scanning the table of contents of this volume, I also noticed an entry for "the seven deadly sins"! *My goodness! Do we even mention such things any more?* Not only that, but there is an entry for "Sins crying to Heaven for Vengeance"! *Oh my! We're so beyond that, aren't we?! How judgmental!* How about this one: "Nine Ways of Being Accessory to Another's Sin". *What?! Am I my brother's keeper?!*

Once again, the thought hits me: we've been robbed. We've had some priceless treasures taken from us: a language (Latin) that adds beauty and a sense of history to our liturgy; music (Gregorian chant) that does the same; a sense of the a sense of the hierarchical nature of the Church (cf. *Lumen gentium*, §18-29; *Sacrosanctum concilium*, §26-32); a sense of the Real Presence of Jesus; a sense of reverence, awe, and wonder associated with the mysteries of the liturgy; a sense of right and wrong; a sense of the power of God; a sense of the importance of our choice of words in speaking to Him; a sense of sin.

But the thief did leave something behind to replace some of the treasures lost: humanity has replaced divinity; "egalitarianism" has replaced the hierarchy; familiarity and contempt have been substituted for reverence, awe, and wonder; "innovation" has replaced tradition; "relevance" has replaced the essential mystery of the liturgy; "tolerance" has replaced our sense of right and wrong; moral relativism has replaced our sense of sin.

We've been robbed. But, thanks be to God, we have a Pope who apparently plans to restore those treasures to the whole Church.

In the letter to bishops accompanying the *motu proprio,* the Holy Father points out that "this Missal was never juridically abrogated and, consequently, in principle, was always permitted," and makes it clear that:

> What earlier generations held as sacred, remains sacred and great for us too, and it cannot be all of a sudden entirely forbidden or even considered harmful. It behooves all of us to preserve the riches which have developed in the Church's faith and prayer, and to give them their proper place.

A Liturgical Bill of Rights

This Liturgical Bill of Rights is excerpted from *Redemptionis Sacramentum*[5] ("On Certain Matters To Be Observed or To Be Avoided Regarding the Most Holy Eucharist," by the Congregation for Divine Worship and Discipline of the Sacraments, March 25, 2004). It's a sort of Reader's Digest Condensed Version, if you will. I present this Bill of Rights here as a reminder of what we are entitled to expect with regard to the liturgy...and even what we are in some instances required to *insist upon* with regard to proper respect for the Most Holy Eucharist. [The bracketed numbers refer to paragraphs in *RS*.]

BY VIRTUE OF THEIR HOLY BAPTISM AND INCORPORATION INTO THE CHURCH, which is the Mystical Body of Christ, each of Christ's Faithful possesses the following rights with respect to the Sacred Liturgy:

1. the right...to a liturgical celebration that is an expression of the Church's life in accordance with her tradition and discipline [11]

2. the right...that the Liturgy, and in particular the celebration of Holy Mass, should truly be as the Church wishes, according to her stipulations as prescribed in the liturgical books and in the other laws and norms [12]

3. the right that the Sacrifice of the Holy Mass should be celebrated for them in an integral manner, according to the entire doctrine of the Church's Magisterium [12]

4. the...right that the celebration of the Most Holy Eucharist should be carried out for it in such a manner that it truly stands out as a

---

[5] "On certain matters to be observed or to be avoided regarding the Most Holy Eucharist" by the Congregation for Divine Worship and Discipline of the Sacraments, 25 March 2004.

sacrament of unity, to the exclusion of all blemishes and actions that might engender divisions and factions in the Church [12][6]

5. the right that ecclesiastical authority should fully and efficaciously regulate the Sacred Liturgy lest it should ever seem to be "anyone's private property, whether of the celebrant or of the community in which the mysteries are celebrated" [18][7]

6. the right...that their diocesan Bishop should take care to prevent the occurrence of abuses in ecclesiastical discipline, especially as regards the ministry of the word, the celebration of the sacraments and sacramentals, the worship of God and devotion to the Saints [24][8]

7. the right...that especially in the Sunday celebration there should customarily be true and suitable sacred music, and that there should always be an altar, vestments and sacred linens that are dignified, proper, and clean, in accordance with the norms [57]

8. the right to a celebration of the Eucharist that has been so carefully prepared in all its parts that:

   • the word of God is properly and efficaciously proclaimed and explained in it
   • the faculty for selecting the liturgical texts and rites is carried out with care according to the norms
   • their faith is duly safeguarded and nourished by the words that are sung in the celebration of the Liturgy [58]

9. [the right] to receive the Eucharist kneeling or standing [91]

---

[6] Cf. 1 Cor 11,17-34; Pope John Paul II, Encyclical Letter, *Ecclesia de Eucharistia*, n. 52: AAS 95 (2003) pp. 467-468.
[7] Cf. Pope John Paul II, Encyclical Letter, *Ecclesia de Eucharistia*, n. 52: AAS 95 (2003) p. 468.
[8] Cf. Code of Canon Law, canon 392.

10. the right to receive Holy Communion on the tongue, at his choice[9]...[or] to receive the Sacrament in the hand[10] [92]

11. a right[11] to visit the Most Holy Sacrament of the Eucharist frequently for adoration, and to take part in adoration before the Most Holy Eucharist exposed at least at some time in the course of any given year [139]

12. [the right] to form guilds or associations for the carrying out of adoration, even almost continuous adoration [141][12]

13. the right...to have the Eucharist celebrated for them on Sunday, and whenever holydays of obligation or other major feasts occur, and even daily insofar as this is possible [162][13]

14. the right, barring a case of real impossibility, that no Priest should ever refuse either to celebrate Mass for the people or to have it celebrated by another Priest if the people otherwise would not be able to satisfy the obligation of participating at Mass on Sunday or the other days of precept [163]

15. the...right that the diocesan Bishop should provide as far as he is able for some celebration to be held on Sundays for that community under his authority and according to the Church's

---

[9] Cf. *Missale Romanum*, Institutio Generalis, n. 161.
[10] But only in areas where the Bishops' Conference with the *recognitio* of the Apostolic See has given permission, such as in the United States of America. Cf. Congregation for Divine Worship and the Discipline of the Sacraments, *Dubium: Notitiæ* 35 (1999) pp. 160-161.
[11] But only where the diocesan Bishop has sacred ministers or others whom he can assign to this purpose.
[12] Cf. Pope John Paul II, Apostolic Constitution, *Pastor Bonus*, art. 65: AAS 80 (1988) p. 877.
[13] "When it is difficult to have the celebration of Mass on a Sunday in a parish church or in another community of Christ's faithful, the diocesan Bishop together with his Priests should consider appropriate remedies. Among such solutions will be that other Priests be called upon for this purpose, or that the faithful transfer to a church in a nearby place so as to participate in the Eucharistic mystery there." [162] Cf. S. Congregation of Rites, Instruction, *Eucharisticum mysterium*, n. 26: AAS 59 (1967) pp. 555-556; Congregation for Divine Worship, Directory for Sunday Celebrations in the Absence of a Priest, *Christi Ecclesia*, 2 June 1988, nn. 5 and 25: *Notitiæ* 24 (1988) pp. 366-378, here pp. 367, 372; n. 18: *Notitiæ* 24 (1988) p. 370.

norms…"[i]f participation at the celebration of the Eucharist is impossible on account of the absence of a sacred minister or for some other grave cause" [164][14]

16. the right to lodge a complaint regarding a liturgical abuse to the diocesan Bishop or the competent Ordinary equivalent to him in law, or to the Apostolic See on account of the primacy of the Roman Pontiff [184][15]

17. [the right to expect that the sacred ministers] fulfill for the faithful those sacred functions that the Church intends to carry out in celebrating the sacred Liturgy at Christ's command [186][16]
.

---

[14] Cf. Code of Canon Law, can. 1248 § 2; Congregation for Divine Worship, Directory for Sunday Celebrations in the Absence of a Priest, Christi Ecclesia, nn. 1-2: Notitiæ 24 (1988) p. 366.
[15] "It is fitting, however, insofar as possible, that the report or complaint be submitted first to the diocesan Bishop. This is naturally to be done in truth and charity." [184]. Cf. Code of Canon Law, can. 1417 § 1: "Because of the primacy of the Roman Pontiff, any of the faithful may either refer their case to, or introduce it before, the Holy See, whether the case be contentious or penal. They may do so at any grade of trial or at any stage of the suit."
[16] Cf. S. Thomas Aquinas, Summa Theol., III, q. 64, a. 9 ad 1. Page 2 of 2.

Section I:
Liturgical Abuse

*The reform that was done, the reform of the rites, went
beyond and in some senses perhaps not completely
coherently, with what the Council Fathers had set forth.
We need to go back and to...not negate everything that
happened, and it's not that everything that happened at the
Council was bad and wrong...but we need to correct the
abuses that entered in and so forth. I have the hope that
some of those elements, for instance, that were taken away
will be reincorporated again, so it will be more evident,
the organic unity of the two forms of the same rite.*

Raymond Cardinal Burke
in a Catholic News Agency video

Liturgical Rights and Liturgical Rites

*Published in **Homiletic and Pastoral Review**, December 2007*. HPR *is now a web-only publication at http://www.hprweb.com.*

Imagine this scenario: On many hot, summer Sunday mornings, Mass begins with Father, the only celebrant, vested in an alb and stole, with no chasuble. A few parishioners are disturbed by this, having a vague feeling that it is "just not right", but they are unsure as to whether or not they are justified in objecting to Father's attire (or lack thereof). Should the parishioners approach Father about this issue, which seems minor to many others of the parish? Or should they simply assume that he has good reason (it's hot, after all!) to refrain from wearing the chasuble?

Before answering these questions, let's consider that many among the laity are finding that they can easily discern whether or not Father's actions are appropriate by way of the internet. For instance, when I have a question about the liturgy, I look through my "Favorites" list and click on my link to the *General Instruction of the Roman Missal* and find an answer. Literally hundreds of Church documents are accessible at www.vatican.va. And, for better or for worse, there are countless blogs making commentary on every issue imaginable, from clergy sexual abuse to liturgical music to the possibility of a universal indult for the Tridentine Mass.

Such easy accessibility of information can be a blessing. Inquiring Catholics can investigate the rich treasury of Church teaching by "googling" in less time than it takes to look up a subject and find the referenced paragraphs in a hard copy of the *Catechism of the Catholic Church*. The internet provides a wonderful opportunity for the laity to educate themselves concerning all that the Catholic

Church believes, professes, and teaches. It helps the faithful fulfill Canon Law:

> Lay people have the duty and the right to acquire the knowledge of Christian teaching which is appropriate to each one's capacity and condition, so that they may be able to live according to this teaching, to proclaim it and if necessary to defend it, and may be capable of playing their part in the exercise of the apostolate. (Canon 229 §1)

Still, it's a two-edged sword for priests. One edge of the sword is that the laity may catechize themselves quite thoroughly on any and all Church issues. This can be a definite boon to pastors, most of whom, as far as I can tell, would like their flocks to have additional catechesis in at least a few areas of religious and spiritual concern. The other edge of the sword, though, is that since the faithful now have increased access to the documents of the Church, they are gaining the ability to notice when things are *not* being done correctly, and this is putting pressure on priests to conform to Church doctrine, teaching, and liturgical procedure.

It seems to me that the most likely area for the faithful to raise questions would be concerning the liturgy. We come together as a parish community at least every Sunday, and liturgical actions are easily observable. Speaking from my own experience, I can say that it is exciting to discover in the *GIRM* a potential for reverence and beauty in the Mass that is not always realized in the *practice* of many parishes. Indeed, the only "perfect" liturgy is the one going on in Heaven, but the Church gives us guidelines and rules that are not whimsical and arbitrary, but rather are meant to increase our reverence for the Mass and enable us to more fully enter into that Heavenly liturgy.

As their knowledge in this area expands, some parishioners will certainly present their concerns about liturgical missteps and abuses to their pastors – as well they should. Sometimes, according to canon law, it is our *duty* to inform our pastors about discrepancies:

> [The faithful] have the right, **indeed at times the duty**, in keeping with their knowledge, competence and position, to manifest to the sacred Pastors their views on matters which concern the good of the Church... (Canon 212, §3, emphasis added)

Parishioners with increasing "knowledge" and "competence" become more and more sensitive to those elements of the Mass that might be poorly executed in their own parish. This increased sensitivity may lead them to "manifest their views" to their pastors.

Now let's return to the scenario described at the beginning of this article: After several weeks of witnessing Father's inappropriate attire, one of the parishioners consults the *GIRM* on-line, and then approaches the priest. He states that he feels this is a liturgical misstep that should be corrected, and mentions the section of the *GIRM* which addresses liturgical vestments.

To the parishioner's surprise and consternation, Father is highly offended, and accuses the parishioner of being "hyper-critical" and "rigid" (it's *hot,* for heaven's sake!).

Obviously, what the faithful consider "manifesting their views" may at times be interpreted as "criticism" by those on the receiving end (the priests) – but is that truly what it is? Fr. Thomas G. Morrow, in his excellent article "The Danger of Criticizing Bishops and Priests" (*HPR*, February 2007), noted the definition of the word "criticize" as "making judgments as to merits and faults" or "to find fault". Fr.

Morrow's point about not judging the personal behavior of a priest or bishop is well-taken. However, when a lay person points out incongruities between, for example, what the *GIRM* specifies as correct liturgical procedure, and what is happening on a regular basis in the parish, this is not, properly speaking, "criticism". Neither is it "finding fault"; rather, it is pointing out an objectively observable error.

To discuss the communication gap that might exist between priest and parishioner, let's back up a couple of steps to examine the first two paragraphs of Canon 212. The first paragraph tells us that

> Christ's faithful, conscious of their own responsibility, are bound to show Christian obedience to what the sacred Pastors, who represent Christ, declare as teachers of the faith and prescribe as rulers of the Church. (Canon 212, §1)

And so, even if the priest is "wrong", a disgruntled lay person may not lead the parish in rebellion! However, courteously informing one's pastor that a particular practice in his parish is not in conformity with the mind of the Church, and asking him to consider rectifying the situation, scarcely amounts to insurrection.

Given that first paragraph of Canon 212, the question may then be asked, can a lay person legitimately raise concerns about certain issues in his/her parish? Certainly such action is permissible! According to the beginning of the second paragraph of Canon 212:

> Christ's faithful are at liberty to make known their needs, especially their spiritual needs, and their wishes to the Pastors of the Church... (Canon 212, §2)

But the second part of this paragraph makes clear that there *is* a difference between "manifesting their views" and "criticizing":

...They have the right also to make their views known to others of Christ's faithful, **but in doing so they must always respect the integrity of faith and morals, show due reverence to the Pastors** and take into account both the common good and the dignity of individuals. (Canon 212, §3, emphasis added)

So the faithful have the right, and at times the duty, to respectfully make their concerns known to their pastors. They do not, however, have the right to offer personal criticism of the pastor, and any communication with the pastor should always be respectful of his authority.

Again, the rub comes when the faithful feel that they have "manifested their views", but the pastor feels "criticized". This is where the sword begins to cut both ways. Due to the limitations of our fallen humanity, some parishioners will be better than others at phrasing their concerns tactfully and leaving personal innuendo out of the issue. And some priests will be more inclined than others to take every point made by a parishioner as a personal criticism of his leadership ability.

Fr. Morrow makes a good point that we should speak "gently" to our priests and bishops about our concerns, and that there are examples among the saints of those who successfully approached the clergy with certain issues. But speaking or writing humbly and respectfully is not a guarantee that one will be heard. While priests and bishops do need our respect, charity, and prayers, this need exists precisely because they are human, and they are not all going to respond positively to even the most gently phrased objection to current practice. Human nature being what it is, even a carefully worded, respectful, and humble letter about liturgical issues might be taken as a criticism by a priest.

For example, I know of a priest who was given the book *Liturgical Question Box* by Monsignor Peter J. Elliott. The book, written in question-and-answer format, has a great deal of useful information. The giver of the gift had no hidden agenda, but thought that the book would be informative and even entertaining for the priest. It became obvious at a daily Mass shortly thereafter, however, that the priest had taken exception to something Monsignor Elliott had written about a liturgical misstep the priest himself was committing, and he made it very clear in his homily that he felt he was being personally criticized. Now, if this priest found Monsignor Elliott's comments personally offensive, I don't know what hope any parishioner will have of communicating a concern to him!

The question of how we can bring our liturgical practice more into line with our liturgical premise may not have occurred to me were it not for the bishop of my diocese issuing a pastoral letter calling for some liturgical corrections. Closely following the publication of that letter, *Redemptionis Sacramentum* was released. Suddenly, it became clear to me that a) there were documents regulating liturgical matters; b) those documents were readily accessible to me, either in printed form or via the internet; and c) current practice was woefully misinformed about correct procedure. Most importantly though, as I read the various documents, I began to see that *correct practice* made the liturgical actions all the more meaningful, all the more reverent, and all the more beautiful. This is what the "right" to good liturgy is all about.

Although most of us would sympathize with a priest or bishop who is beset by rude and disrespectful complaints about liturgical errors, our pastoral leaders still have a duty to remedy an abuse, if it exists. Even a poorly expressed concern, if it addresses a valid point, must be investigated because "Christ's faithful have the right that ecclesiastical authority should fully and efficaciously regulate the

Sacred Liturgy..."(*RS*, §18). The Church charges the diocesan bishop with the role of "moderator, promoter and guardian of [the Church's] whole liturgical life" (*RS*, §19), and gives priests the command to "go to the trouble of properly cultivating their liturgical knowledge and ability" (*RS*, §33) so as to ensure proper worship by the faithful.

Unfortunately, parish priests are often caught in the middle between those who seek a liturgy more in conformity with the mind of the Church, and those who are quite attached to "the way we've always done it." A priest may fear that if he makes changes in favor of the correct norms, he will alienate the vocal minority who feel that they are operating according to "the spirit of Vatican II". But the way to care for the souls of these mistaken parishioners is to gently guide them to a better understanding of the liturgy and the need for the "rules and regulations" that increase our sense of reverence.

It can be very discouraging to the faithful to find that liturgical practice in their parish does not conform to the standards set by the Church, After all, *Redemptionis Sacramentum* assures us that:

> ...it is the right of all of Christ's faithful that the Liturgy, and in particular the celebration of Holy Mass, should truly be as the Church wishes, according to her stipulations as prescribed in the liturgical books and in the other laws and norms. Likewise, the Catholic people have the right that the Sacrifice of the Holy Mass should be celebrated for them in an integral manner, according to the entire doctrine of the Church's Magisterium. Finally, it is the Catholic community's right that the celebration of the Most Holy Eucharist should be carried out for it in such a manner that it truly stands out as a sacrament of unity, to the exclusion of

all blemishes and actions that might engender divisions and factions in the Church. (*RS*, §12)

It is even more discouraging to find, as is sometimes the case, that the pastor has little or no inclination to make the necessary changes. Again, *Redemptionis Sacramentum* speaks to the issue:

> The Mystery of the Eucharist "is too great for anyone to permit himself to treat it **according to his own whim**, so that its sacredness and its universal ordering would be obscured". On the contrary, anyone who acts thus by giving free reign to his own inclinations, **even if he is a Priest**, injures the substantial unity of the Roman Rite, which ought to be vigorously preserved, and becomes responsible for actions that are in no way consistent with the hunger and thirst for the living God that is experienced by the people today. **Nor do such actions serve authentic pastoral care** or proper liturgical renewal; instead, they deprive Christ's faithful of their patrimony and their heritage. (*RS*, §11, emphasis added)

And it is more discouraging yet to find oneself being reproached for being "rigid" and "too 'by-the-book'" when *Redemptionis Sacramentum* insists that

> …the structures and forms of the sacred celebrations according to each of the Rites of both East and West are in harmony with the practice of the universal Church also as regards practices received universally from apostolic and unbroken tradition, which it is the Church's task to transmit faithfully and carefully to future generations. **All these things are wisely safeguarded and protected by the liturgical norms.** (*RS*, §9, emphasis added)

In other words, there *is* a "book" and we are *required* to "go by" it.

One priest of my acquaintance, when confronted with liturgical concerns, has said, on several occasions, "You are correct. But sometimes there are more important things than being right." Pastoral concerns are one thing, but a comment such as this effectively removes the topic – whatever it may be – from the realm of rational discussion by reducing the truth to relativism. The person making the statement ascribes to himself the ability to determine when it is appropriate to be "right" (i.e., to conform to liturgical norms) and when there are "more important" concerns. Again, *Redemptionis Sacramentum* corrects this misconception:

> ...For **arbitrary actions** are not conducive to true renewal, but **are detrimental** to the right of Christ's faithful to a liturgical celebration that is an expression of the Church's life in accordance with her tradition and discipline. In the end, they introduce elements of distortion and disharmony into the very celebration of the Eucharist, which is oriented in its own lofty way and by its very nature to signifying and wondrously bringing about the communion of divine life and the unity of the People of God. **The result is uncertainty in matters of doctrine, perplexity and scandal** on the part of the People of God, and, almost as a necessary consequence, vigorous opposition, **all of which greatly confuse and sadden many of Christ's faithful** in this age of ours when Christian life is often particularly difficult on account of the inroads of "secularization" as well. (*RS*, §11, emphasis added)

Our priests and bishops cannot have it both ways: if they want the laity to be better educated and to rise to new spiritual levels in their faith life, they must be willing to hear the concerns of people who question erroneous liturgical practices in their own parishes. If a priest feels he is being criticized, one solution might be to appoint those members of the laity who seem to have a growing knowledge of liturgical correctness to the parish liturgy committee. That way, those interested in experiencing a liturgy that is in conformity with the norms established by the Church would be able to put their knowledge into practice – and the priest may come to feel that these "critics" are now working *with* him instead of *against* him.

Of course, the laity, for all their rights to express their concerns, should do so respectfully and humbly; but there will be times when they don't. Even at those times, though, our priests and bishops, who are our leaders, are called by the Church to *listen*:

> … Let Bishops, Priests and Deacons, in the exercise of the sacred ministry, examine their consciences as regards the authenticity and fidelity of the actions they have performed in the name of Christ and the Church in the celebration of the Sacred Liturgy. **Let each one of the sacred ministers ask himself, even with severity, whether he has respected the rights of the lay members** of Christ's faithful, who confidently entrust themselves and their children to him, relying on him to fulfill for the faithful those sacred functions that the Church intends to carry out in celebrating the sacred Liturgy at Christ's command. **For each one should always remember that he is a servant of the Sacred Liturgy.** (*RS*, §186, emphasis added)

Let us all strive for and pray for charitable and fruitful exchanges between clergy and laity about liturgical (and other) concerns. Let us pray for leadership from our bishops and priests which will bring unity to groups within the laity who differ in their understanding of the liturgy.

Finally, let us pray for increased understanding among both laity and clergy of the importance and significance of the guidelines and norms established by the Church for protecting the sacred nature of the Mass.

Sweating the Small Stuff

I'm sure you've heard this one: "Rule Number One is, don't sweat the small stuff. Rule Number Two is, it's all small stuff." That may be a workable adage for earthly matters, but not for spiritual concerns. In the Kingdom, everything is turned upside down: the meek shall inherit the earth; when I am weak, then I am strong; we must die to self in order to truly live. In the Kingdom, sometimes the "small stuff" is the truly important stuff. And in the Kingdom, it's definitely *not* all "small stuff".

Concerning the liturgy, the "little things" spelled out in the rubrics or in Canon Law or in the *General Instruction of the Roman Missal* (*GIRM*) are all there for a reason, and the net effect of a correct implementation of each part is a more beautiful portrait of the Heavenly Banquet. In his book *Worship as a Revelation*, Laurence Paul Hemming states,

> A further part of this textual character of the liturgy as a whole is the vestments the furnishing and ordering of the church interior, the shape and character of the sacred vessels, the materials from which all is made, its exact placing and so forth. **Everything in a church intends a meaning**, so that the whole of the liturgy, its chant, what is performed, by whom, and how, where, and when, form a **whole textual complex with intricate significance**. (p. 11)

It seems to me that the average Catholic – the one who goes to Mass on Sunday and maybe holy days of obligation (wait…is that really average these days?) – well, anyway, the average Catholic: a) doesn't know what the rubrics say about how the liturgy is supposed to be celebrated; b) doesn't care; and c) is fine with keeping things just as they are. "This is how we've always done it", and they don't want anything to change.

The result is that – at least where I live – we have Catholic parishes that look, act, and think more like Protestant churches: the focus of worship is more human-centered – it's all about "us". The music is "what makes us feel good". The homilies are pabulum (actually, a lot of Protestant homilists are serving meat, while many Catholic priests stick to cereal). We want to be "inclusive" and make people feel "comfortable".

The liturgy is too significant to take lightly or to meddle with unnecessarily: It is "the summit toward which the activity of the Church is directed; it is also the fount from which all her power flows" (*Sacrosanctum Concilium*, §10). It is the source and summit of our life as Christians (*Lumen Gentium*, §11). It is the earthly sign of the heavenly banquet and our communion with the saints: "In the earthly liturgy we take part in a foretaste of that heavenly liturgy which is celebrated in the Holy City of Jerusalem toward which we journey as pilgrims…" (*SC*, §8). What can possibly be "small" in such an important piece of our Catholic Christian identity?

Here's a list of some of the "small stuff" that bothers me at Mass:

- Sloppily attired altar servers

- "Contemporary" music

- Priest adding "Good morning" at the beginning of the liturgy, and "Have a nice day" at the end

- Inappropriate items placed on the altar

- Using the altar as a background for "seasonal" decorations

And here's a list of some of the "big stuff" that makes me cringe:

- Priest adlibbing the Lamb of God and/or any other prayers

- Calling for "spontaneous" general intercessions

- Inappropriate vestments

- Lay ministers performing tasks that should be reserved to priests, deacons, or acolytes

- Unvested lay ministers entering the sanctuary to receive Holy Communion

- Acolytes and deacons performing tasks that should be reserved to priests

These are just a few examples, and you may agree or disagree as to whether they are "small stuff" or "big stuff". To me, frankly, they're all "big stuff". These errors violate the sacred structure of the Mass, disdain tradition and apostolic teaching, and contribute to a general lack of reverence for the liturgy.

The point is, in the liturgy, we *need* to sweat *all* of the "stuff" in order to make sure that the big picture is not out of focus.

But my view is not shared by many in the parishes I've experienced. An entirely different attitude prevails: one of casualness. One parishioner asked me in all sincerity, "Do you really think that stuff matters to God?" She also wondered aloud why my opinion on liturgical matters should matter more than hers or some other parishioners'. My explanation that it was not *my opinion*, but rather, what the Church demands of us for *Her* liturgy, fell on deaf ears. This parishioner – and she's not the only one – has no concept of the authority of Church teaching, documents, or tradition. She doesn't know the difference between an encyclical and an encyclopedia, or between the *GIRM* and the missalette ("Isn't everything we need to know in the missalette?" she inquired).

Another parishioner told me he didn't understand why we should have to follow a bunch of rules about the way the sanctuary was furnished and how the altar was covered. "I think people should be comfortable when they come to church," he said.

Sadly, this comment is probably the most telling of all. I would say that people are definitely "comfortable" in our Catholic churches. They are so comfortable that they feel free to traipse through the sanctuary at will, with a quick nod of the head toward the tabernacle. They feel comfortable enough to enter the sanctuary and stand right next to the altar to receive Holy Communion. The altar servers feel comfortable enough to slouch and yawn their way through Mass. The priests are comfortable enough to treat their role as one of talk-show host. Once, I suggested to a priest that if Jesus entered the room, we would all fall on our faces in adoration, not just greet him with a casual, "Oh, hi, Lord." He laughed and said he would probably do the latter.

In truth, most priests probably do follow the rubrics quite well... or at least intend to. For most, any errors are probably due to oversight or ignorance, rather than blatant disobedience. Busy parish priests may find it difficult to take the time to study the *GIRM*. However, shouldn't this have been covered in the seminary?!

I also understand that priests are faced with "parishioner pressure" – those pillars of the local parish community who tell the priest, "But this is the way we've *always* done it". And certainly, re-catechizing such parishioners can be a daunting task. In my own little parish, I have had unfruitful conversations with others regarding liturgical issues.

But I think priests and bishops are making a big mistake by "going with the flow" in their parishes and dioceses. If they are not moving toward greater liturgical excellence, then they're going backwards. And they are doing a disservice to the faithful.

When priests and bishops dismiss liturgical abuses as insignificant they do two things: First of all, they allow the faithful to persist in their errors, and hand these errors on to the next generation of parishioners ("that's how we've always done it"). They dilute our Catholic identity.

Second, they cause scandal. When a faithful Catholic discovers the truth about the liturgy, he's bound to wonder why the shepherds of the Church have failed to teach it. When a faithful Catholic begins to see the beauty, wisdom, majesty, and pure depth of Catholic tradition, he is bound to wonder why the shepherds of the Church have hidden it.

And he begins to wonder if those shepherds are really wolves in sheep's clothing. That is not a good thing.

Personally, I've been maligned by the pastor of my own parish (and beyond) mainly because of my orthodox views. I've been censured by an acting bishop. So what I see is that the leadership of the Church cares very little about the liturgy, but very much about popular opinion. And since my "opinion" is not popular, they don't care about it.

It doesn't bother me that the powers-that-be (or even my friends, family, and fellow parishioners) don't care about my "opinions". Sometimes, I don't care about theirs, either! What bothers me is that they are so quick to dismiss what the Church has to say about the liturgy and how it should be celebrated. This is not a matter of opinion, and shouldn't be dismissed as such. It is a matter of truth.

When people say the rubrics are optional or don't matter for some reason or another, what they are really saying is that *their* opinion should hold sway. They tell me I'm too "rigid". To them, I offer this thought from Pope Benedict XVI, writing as Cardinal Joseph Ratzinger:

> The life of the liturgy does not come from what dawns upon the minds of individuals and planning groups…[It] becomes personal, true, and new, **not through tomfoolery and banal experiments with the words**, but through a courageous entry into the great reality that through the rite is always ahead of us and can never quite be overtaken.
>
> Does it still need to be explicitly stated that all **this has nothing to do with rigidity**? *(Spirit of the Liturgy*, p. 168)

Liturgical Abuse at First Holy Communion

This guest commentary was provided by a good friend of mine, who describes the liturgical abuse she observed at her granddaughter's First Holy Communion.

Attending a First Communion event in the Archdiocese of Portland never promised to be a walk in the park, but what it turned out to be was a "Catholic" fiasco of the stuff of nightmares. The presence of a Buddhist prayer wheel could not have made it more alien to my understanding of the Church's worship.

The preparation for my granddaughter's reception of the Eucharist proceeded well. A princess by temperament, she chose a tiara to wear with her veil. Her dress was a lacy confection previously worn by her mom and her cousin. How sweet, right? Until the big day actually dawned...
The parish in question shall remain nameless, but it is representative of many in Oregon's largest city. The priest, appropriately named Father "Pete," is in his 50's, tall and imposing, but obviously a marshmallow inside, whose primary reading material must consist entirely of the least challenging juvenile literature.

The day began with the obligatory picture-taking – which went on for the better part of an hour, inside and outside the sanctuary. Well, parents and grandparents can be excused for this bit of sentimentality, even if it celebrates the fancy clothes and nervous smiles more than it acknowledges the momentous fact of initiation into the reception of Christ Himself.

During the photo shoot, however, a full church of early attendees – hoping to be seated where they could take yet more pictures of Johnny and Susie in the very act of Eucharistic reception – visited freely and loudly. In a lifetime in the Catholic Church, I have never seen a crowd act more like they were at cocktail party, instead of in the presence of the Blessed Sacrament – conveniently assigned to a side altar, and apparently ignored. And on this occasion, a first was achieved for me: watching the godparents of my granddaughter bring their cups of Starbucks' designer coffee into the church – and drink it in the aisles and in the pew before Mass. The smell of latte lingered long after they had stopped consuming the brew – barely in time for the processional.

I breathed a sigh of relief when the choir finally assembled – a dozen people of all ages and both sexes, who found a place ten feet from the altar in the sanctuary – so that at least the noise subsided to a dull roar. The singers looked harmless enough with their OCP books, but the bongos some of them held make me cringe. Shortly after the tuning up ended, the lector admonished us to "introduce yourselves to your neighbors." My hope was that this pre-liturgical action would replace the "sign of peace" glad-handing. No such luck; that little "ritual" took place later in the long event and lasted five minutes

Then we all rose and gawked at the 30-some kids in their finery, as the procession started. I didn't count the verses of the "gathering song" (at least seven) as the first communicants preceded an army of servers of both sexes, lectors (although the youngsters did all the readings except the Gospel), extraordinary ministers (mostly women), and, finally, Father Pete, attired in a fairly standard chasuble, but adorned with colors not listed in the rubrics. I had never laid eyes on him before and was to soon wish I never would again.

Once the choir finally shut up, Father proceeded to poll the crowd about who came the farthest for the occasion. Connecticut won up front, but he continued to acknowledge folks from Illinois, Utah, and even The Dalles [Oregon]. Then he launched into the new translation prayers, many of which received the wrong responses and were punctuated by his ad-libbing, but then the Mass had already begun to seem irrelevant in the face of all the personal "sharing."

After more insights inserted by the celebrant, who didn't seem to want to stop talking long enough to actually say the Mass, the sung Gloria began. Father then proceeded to go up and down the church aisles, sprinkling everyone heavily with holy water. As the time for the readings approached, several youngsters in white and black lined up to render Scripture (three in turn on a reading, lest anyone be too taxed), and sing the Responsorial Psalm. After that painful interlude – soon to be followed by many more – the celebrant hoisted the book of Scripture, marched to the back of the church, **unattended** by his phalanx of servers and candle bearers, and told us all to turn around for the Gospel. Huh?!

The homily gave the best intimation of how much worse it would get. After gathering all the children to sit with him at the base of the altar, our celebrant took out a basket and held up "bread," in this case hamburger and hot dog buns, and asked the children what they were and what made them special. Well, of course, he finally summarized, it was the "fixin's" – meat and ketchup or mustard – that were important. Then he reached to the bottom of the basket for some hosts. These too were bread, he elicited from the eight-year-olds, but in this case, the "fixin's" came from the Holy Spirit. I finally shut out the rest of the pre-school catechesis and prayed I could hang on and not make a scene.

It got worse. After the Creed, which took less time than the comments about our Baptismal promises leading up to it, we got to the Offertory, which evoked a procession of a dozen youngsters carrying nothing, and a line of more to say the prayers of the faithful. All this time the choir was singing the contemporary version of *Ubi Caritas*, while women filled the numerous chalices on the altar, and

Father relaxed after his efforts at setting up an atmosphere of conviviality. Father then took a huge beaker of wine and some glass chalices into the congregation and had the children pour the wine into them.

When time for the Preface arrived, Father once again invited the entire group of first communicants to stand around him at the altar and hold hands. This lasted *through the consecration*, which seemed to be taking place as the celebrant held the host and then the chalice down at the children's level, turning in a circle, *while saying the words of transubstantiation!* I resolved at that point to abstain from the sacrament, since its validity appeared in question.

I lasted until the children's Communion, which took place with Father **seated** on the lowest step; Communion was given *only in the hand*, followed by a drink from the chalice held by – who else? – a woman. It had been explained to me earlier that it was fine for the children to drink the Precious Blood from the chalice because they had been given a taste of the unconsecrated wine days before, so "they wouldn't spit it out in disgust during Mass." Oh, well, that's okay, then.

Although I had to tread on a few feet, I managed to get out of there as the congregation began to line up for Communion, pleading my bad hip, which had indeed begun to throb agonizingly. I hid out in the car until I heard, to my surprise, an organ play the recessional. Yes, the church has a beautiful organ and evidently someone who can play it. But flutes, tambourines, and pianos are so much more *relevant,* don'tcha know?

After Mass, one person in our party from out-of-town, whom I had been told attended a Latin Mass regularly and *loved it* – said to me, "That was the most beautiful First Communion I have ever seen!" I tried not to wince, went on auto pilot, and figured I would be able to leave soon. I managed to get to an exit point without meeting Father

"Pete" formally (my hip did not allow me to walk all the way across the church hall to where he was), thus avoiding the sin of striking – or at the very least, cussing out – a priest.

If this is business as usual for the "Oregon Church," God help us all. Pray a new prelate soon arrives in Portland[17] and stops this obscene use of the liturgy as an occasion to glorify ~~man~~ (oops!) *persons.*

[17] This article describes a Mass that took place prior to the arrival of Archbishop Alexander King Sample in April 2013.

Blessings at Communion

In 2012, I was heartened as a couple of bishops made the headlines by correcting some liturgical abuses: Bishop Robert C. Morlino of the Diocese of Madison, Wisconsin, adhering to the established norms of offering only the Body of Christ, and not the Precious Blood, at Holy Communion; Bishop Thomas J. Olmsted of the Diocese of Phoenix, Arizona doing the same, and also accepting only male altar servers in his Cathedral. (As an added bonus, limiting reception of Holy Communion to one species also ends up correcting the error of having multitudes of lay ministers administering the chalice.)

This all puts me in mind of another abuse that I find particularly offensive: a communion procession interspersed with ***non-***communicants who approach the priest or extraordinary minister for a "blessing" instead of receiving Holy Communion. It's certainly not an unfamiliar experience in the Catholic Church in the United States. In fact, one priest of my acquaintance regularly gives these instructions just before Communion: "If you have not received your first Communion, or you are not disposed to receive Communion, please place your hand over your heart and you may receive a blessing. ***Everyone is welcome at the table of the Lord!***"

Of course, I suppose we can acknowledge that while there is nothing in the rubrics to indicate that a blessing should or may be given to non-communicants during Holy Communion, neither is there any explicit prohibition of the practice.

However, in November 2008, a letter from the Congregation for Divine Worship and the Discipline of the Sacraments[18] surfaced on the internet regarding this conferral of a "blessing" to non-

---

[18] See Appendix A

communicants at Mass during Holy Communion. The letter was a response to an inquiry which consisted of two questions:

1. Is this a custom that is within the faculty of a pastor, the local Ordinary, or a Bishops' Conference to establish? That is, is this custom something that can be regulated without recourse to this Congregation?

2. Are there particular guidelines or restrictions from this Congregation concerning a) which ministers of Holy Communion may give these blessings and b) what forms these blessings may take?

The letter from the CDW stated, in part:

1. The liturgical blessing of the Holy Mass is properly given to each and to all at the conclusion of the Mass, just a few moments subsequent to the distribution of Holy Communion.

2. Lay people, within the context of Holy Mass, are unable to confer blessings. These blessings, rather, are the competence of the priest (cf. *Ecclesia de Mysterio*, Notitiae 34 (15 Aug. 1997), art. 6, § 2; can. 1169, § 2; and Roman Ritual De Benedictionibus (1985), n. 18).

3. Furthermore, the laying on of a hand or hands – which has its own sacramental significance, inappropriate here – by those distributing Holy Communion, in substitution for its reception, is to be explicitly discouraged.

4. The Apostolic Exhortation *Familiaris Consortio*, n. 84, "forbids any pastor, for whatever reason or pretext even of a pastoral nature, to perform ceremonies of any kind for divorced people who remarry." To be feared is that any form of blessing in substitution for communion would give the impression that the divorced and remarried have been

returned, in some sense, to the status of Catholics in good standing.

5. In a similar way, for others who are not to be admitted to Holy Communion in accord with the norm of law, the Church's discipline has already made clear that they should not approach Holy Communion nor receive a blessing. This would include non-Catholics and those envisaged in can. 915 (i.e., those under the penalty of excommunication or interdict, and others who obstinately persist in manifest grave sin).

The intent here seems pretty clear to me: liturgical actions are kept in proper order both within the liturgy and according to the competence of the ministers; erroneous impressions of approval are avoided; and Holy Communion is recognized for what it is.

At the time the letter came out, I shared it with lay people and priests – and met with scoffing and sarcasm from most. One friend asked, "Are we as lay people not to say 'God bless you' when someone sneezes?" From priests, I heard comments that tried to show "pastoral prudence", such as: "How can we deny people a blessing *which they have come to expect?*" and "People will be upset and might leave the Church!" Or this one (see my eyes rolling?): "If we deny them a blessing, we are not showing them *love*, and after all, *what would Jesus do?!* Surely he would not deny them!"

The CDW letter, even if not "official", still contained a clear statement that giving a "blessing" at Communion is inappropriate. But the fall-back position of several priests I spoke to, who objected to the idea of denying the blessing, seemed to be: "I'm not changing anything until I'm explicitly told I have to." I do know one priest who was willing to withhold the blessing; he was told by his bishop that he must give it! Sigh. I think that the "spirit of Vatican II" is alive and well, while the spirit of obedience to authority is pitiably lacking!

What surprises me the most is that most of the people I have mentioned this to seem to be completely unaware of the underlying message that the "blessing at Communion" sends. The CDW letter mentions it briefly: "To be feared is that any form of blessing in substitution for communion" might give the wrong impression.

I would argue that indeed it does give the wrong impression, and has for many years – so strongly that it has detracted from the belief in the Real Presence of Jesus in the Blessed Sacrament; it has detracted from our sense of sin; and it has convinced us that it is not really so urgent that we go to confession. Four years after the CDW letter came out, nothing has changed in *my* diocese.

Hmph! Well, I think this calls for a limerick:

> The faithful want to be blessed,
> Because they haven't confessed.
> Rome says not to.
> The bishop says "got to" --
> Just as one would've guessed.

> If the offended should all leave the Church,
> The bishop'll be in the lurch.
> There won't be enough money!
> That wouldn't be funny.
> It would require a new funding search.

> They won't change the wrong for the right,
> Or the "faithful" will exit in fright.
> Pastors stick with the wrong
> To maintain the throng,
> And we end up with Katholic-Lite

Altar *Boys*: There's a Good Reason for That

A correspondent sent me the following wonderful news in an email the other day:

> After Mass yesterday, Father asked for a few moments of our time. He announced that one of the young men who serve during the Mass is entering the seminary next week.
>
> The young man then gave a brief talk. He had discovered the Latin Mass about 5 years ago and started attending. Father is very good at spotting new faces in the crowd, and after a few Masses, he suggested to the young man that if he wanted a greater understanding of Our Lord, then he might consider serving at the altar.
>
> The young man thought about it, then agreed. He was given some instruction, and was allowed to serve during the Low Mass. Eventually he served at the High Mass.
>
> He didn't know Latin when he began, but as we know, it's something that grows on you.
>
> The young man acknowledged the influence that serving has had on his decision to answer the Call. It was the proximity to God, among other things. The young man also called for other boys and men in the community to step up. He said that it's a privilege available to all baptized Catholic men, and one that should be taken advantage of.

Interestingly, on the same day, I received an email from another correspondent alerting me to an article in the 2/9/12 on-line edition of *The Wanderer:* "The Anomaly of 'Altar Girls'", by Fr. Brian W. Harrison, OS.

The article is well worth reading in its entirety. I point here to a few paragraphs which mesh nicely with the story related above. First, Fr. Harrison points out the lack of precedent for female altar servers (all **emphases** mine):

> It must be said in the first place that the absolute novelty of female altar service practice is in itself troubling. For when a given liturgical custom has not only existed, but has been continuously and **emphatically reaffirmed and insisted upon since the patristic era**, there must be a presumption that such a custom is very probably Apostolic in origin, reflecting the will — a marked preference or even a requirement — of Christ Himself.

> In the Vatican journal *Notitiæ* (Vol. 16, 1980), the liturgical scholar Aimé-Georges Martimort … goes on to quote Pope St. Gelasius in 494, who wrote to the bishops of Sicily and southern Italy: "We have heard with **sorrow of the great contempt with which the sacred mysteries have been treated**. It has reached the point where women have been encouraged to serve at the altar, and to carry out roles that are not suited to their sex, having been assigned exclusively to those of masculine gender."

> Every edition of the Roman Missal **from 1570 till 1962 carried the prohibition of female altar service**, as did the 1917 Code of Canon Law (c. 813, §2), not to mention the earlier documents of the postconciliar liturgical reform itself.

> But if the emphatic and uninterrupted tradition of the Church reserved the sanctuary, and especially the altar itself, for ministers of the male sex, **what was the main reason for this?** Many have noted that the admission of "altar girls" often has the effect of **discouraging young boys from a**

service no longer seen as masculine in character, so that a fruitful source of future priestly vocations is thereby placed at risk. It has also been pointed out that a further obstacle is posed by this innovation to reunion with the Eastern Orthodox, who roundly reject it.

But such objections do not get to the heart of the matter, which is pinpointed by Martimort as ". . . the link which was understood to **unite the lesser ministries to the priesthood itself, to the point where they had become the normal stages leading to the priesthood.** This link is already present in the perspective of St. Cyprian [d. 258]."

Thus, the Church's unwillingness from time immemorial to have females acting at the altar has clearly been linked to the fact that **altar service is closely related to the ministerial priesthood,** which, as John Paul II reaffirmed definitively in *Ordinatio Sacerdotalis,* **can never possibly be conferred upon women.**

Fr. Harrison also presents his opinion that it is not objectionable to have females serve as readers or extraordinary ministers of Holy Communion. He points out the fallacy of an "all or nothing" scenario – the notion that females must be given either unrestricted access to liturgical service, or none at all. The important factor is whether the ministry is seen as leading to the priesthood.

There are precedents dating back to the patristic era for the reading of the Epistle (sometimes even the Gospel), and for the administration of Communion under extraordinary circumstances, to be carried out by **persons not seen as in any way as being on the road to the priesthood.** Altar service, on the other hand, has **always traditionally been envisaged as something strictly reserved for those with**

the potential to become priests; and precisely for that reason it has been permitted to young boys as well as more mature males.

The server is **presented visually and symbolically in that role by his male, clerical dress (cassock and surplice), by his location at the altar, and by his actions**, which provide proximate assistance and preparation for the **quintessentially priestly act**: the offering of the Eucharistic Sacrifice.

But in recent years the Latin-Rite Church, by inviting females to serve at the place of priestly sacrifice dressed in the sacerdotal garb of alb or cassock, seems to be speaking with a forked tongue. At the level of her purely **verbal** communication the **Church promulgates documents excluding women's ordination irrevocably**; but in her "**body language**" during the Eucharist — her most sacred liturgical *action* — she is now **insinuating the exact opposite**. The presence of female servers at the altar is a **silent but eloquent challenge to the Church's infallible teaching that women can never be priests.**

I think the story at the beginning of this post of the young man who has answered the call to the priesthood due largely to his service at the altar aptly illustrates the significance of Fr. Harrison's historical analysis. Serving at the altar *is* an important "stepping stone" toward the priesthood.

Fr. Harrison also points out that:

> …the Congregation for Divine Worship ruled in 2001 that **no bishop may *require* any of his priests to celebrate with female servers. Male only** altar service is described as a "**noble tradition**" which is "**always very appropriate.**"

…

… Female altar service is a novelty that clearly will not be rolled back overnight; so at this early stage, the best scenario would be one in which an increasing number of priests – and, hopefully, bishops – show themselves **willing to face down the predictable opposition and lead by personal example, returning to the practice of celebrating with male servers only**. And they will be greatly assisted in doing that if **increasing numbers of lay Catholics (of both sexes) openly support and encourage them in this initiative**.

Perhaps it wouldn't hurt to just make a friendly comment to your own parish priest in this regard; simply making a positive comment about the *presence* of male altar servers (if there are any!), rather than a negative one about female altar servers, could make the point in a non-abrasive way. Priests who know they can count on some support will certainly be more likely to make the change.

Priests need that support from the laity because they don't always get it from their bishops. In response to a dubium submitted by a bishop to the *Congregation for Divine Worship and the Discipline of the Sacraments* on whether a bishop had the authority to compel his priests to employ the use of females to serve at the altar, the then-Prefect, Cardinal Medina Estevez replied in 2001 in the negative. In explaining this, he concluded: "Therefore, in the event that Your Excellency found it opportune to authorize service of women at the altar, **it would remain important to explain clearly to the faithful the nature of this innovation**, lest confusion might be introduced, thereby **hampering the development of priestly vocations**." (July 27, 2001; Prot. 2451/00/L[19], **emphases** added)

[19] http://www.catholicliturgy.com/index.cfm/FuseAction/DocumentContents/ DocumentIndex/556

In doing so he was merely restating the provisions of the 1994 Circular Letter to the Presidents of the Episcopal Conferences[20] on this issue, in which it was decreed:

1) Canon 230 #2 has a *permissive* and not a *preceptive* character: *Laici . . . possunt.* Hence the permission given in this regard by some Bishops can in no way be considered as binding on other Bishops. In fact, it is the competence of each Bishop, in his diocese, after hearing the opinion of the Episcopal Conference, to make a prudential judgment on what to do, with a view to the ordered development of liturgical life in his own diocese.

2) The Holy See respects the decision adopted by certain Bishops for *specific* local reasons on the basis of the provisions of Canon 230 2. At the same time, however, the Holy See wishes to recall that it will always be very appropriate to follow the noble tradition of having boys serve at the altar. As is well known, this has led to a reassuring development of priestly vocations. Thus the obligation to support such groups of altar boys will always continue.

3) If in some diocese, on the basis of Canon 230 #2, the Bishop permits that, for *particular* reasons, women may also serve at the altar, *this decision must be clearly explained to the faithful*, in the light of the above-mentioned norm. It shall also be made clear that the norm is already being widely applied, by the fact that women frequently serve as lectors in the Liturgy and can also be called upon to distribute Holy Communion as Extraordinary Ministers of the Eucharist and to carry out other functions, according to the provisions of the same Canon 230 #3.

---

[20] http://www.ewtn.com/library/CURIA/CDWCOMM.HTM

4) It must also be clearly understood that the liturgical services mentioned above are carried out by lay people *ex temporanea deputatione*, according to the judgment of the Bishop, without lay people, be they men or women, having any right to exercise them.

The two requirements for employing the use of women and girls to serve at the altar - a) that it be done only for specific reasons ["equal opportunity" is not a valid reason] and b) that the decision be clearly explained to the faithful – have, to quote Hamlet, been "more honour'd in the breach than the observance" (Act 1, Scene 4). In my experience, I know of not a single bishop who has fulfilled these requirements in permitting the use of female altar servers.

Secondly, to the specific situation in my own diocese, the Diocese of Baker: in the nineteen years since the publication of that 1994 Circular Letter, our Diocese has seen only two native sons ordained to the priesthood for the Diocese (there is, possibly, a third, but I am not certain as to whether he fits into that time frame). While our Diocese has never known an abundance of vocations to the priesthood, it would seem that there is some correlation between the introduction of the use of female altar servers in our Diocese and the near catastrophic decline in native vocations since that date.

The Lighter Side: Attire at Mass

An email correspondent tells me that a certain parish in our diocese, which shall remain nameless at the moment, seems to have a less-than-orthodox view of proper dress for the faithful at Mass.

I've edited her comments just a bit, but here's what she told me:

> We have men in shorts and flip-flops presenting the Eucharist at all of our "too many to count Masses". God doesn't care what we wear, or that we're eating and drinking and texting during Mass; He just wants us to be happy...Oh, really? They must think He wears a red suit with a black belt and boots when He comes down from heaven on Christmas morning. Now you've done it, Jay, are you happy? My blood pressure is now up.

> I grew up in Boston and we spent every summer on Cape Cod. Even though we spent every day in shorts and sandals, we always dressed for Church, or we weren't allowed in. If my mom can dress seven kids with dresses, gloves, and hats, and with patent leather shoes (white for summer), the adults at [our parish] should be able to dress for the Altar. It's disgraceful.

> When we ask individuals to show the same respect to God that they would show their bosses at work, we are told God doesn't care what we wear as long as we show up.

> As far as dressing for Mass goes, we should hold a fundraiser for the worst, most inappropriate dress, Diocese-wide; [my parish] would win hands down and if everyone had to pay a dollar to enter the contest, we could pay off our note [on the new church].

The other day, I tapped the shoulder of the father of a teenage girl and asked him what he was thinking about the length [or lack thereof!] of his daughter's skirt. He told me to ask her mother, but I said, "No, I am asking you. You're her father, and you are supposed to watch out for her where her mother fails." Then I asked him to give the girl his jacket and cover her up, and he did.

Once we had a lector bring her 10-12-year old daughter up to the ambo to read (a task too great for this poor child; what do they teach in public school instead of reading?)…where was I…oh, she had on flip-flops and a sarong over a wet bathing suit. So please, Jay, don't tell me about the short shorts at your parish; those were our "good ol' days". Once, I was at Mass in [a neighboring parish] when the priest stopped the Communion procession and told the women to please wear underwear, that he was also a man. How awful.

Indeed!

My correspondent also had a few comments about the two churches in the parish. The old church is lovely, but was too small, I guess, for the growing congregation, so a new one was built at a hefty expense. She notes

> We call the Downtown Church, the Traditional Church; it's officially known as the Historic Church. We call the "new" church the Armadillo, because from the top it looks like one.

The contingent that likes the traditional church has come forward with funds to restore some of the "renovated" aspects. My correspondent says:

> Father has received some donations to fix up the traditional church, and it's looking pretty good. I love that church. We are looking for a Communion rail. The original one was cut

up and neighbors to the church placed the pieces they acquired on their front porches many years ago.

That makes me weep!

But the conclusion of our email conversation on the subject brought tears to my eyes for a different reason. I had responded to one message by simply writing, "ROFL!" A quick response asked, "What does that mean?" and I explained, "**R**olling **O**n the **F**loor **L**aughing. And LOL means **L**aughing **O**ut **L**oud." Later, this note arrived in my inbox:

> Thanks. I was told by my daughter that LOL means lots of love, so all this time I was wondering if you and I were having a moment. I can't tell you how glad I am that you cleared things up.

Glimmers of Hope, Part I

A Glimmer of Hope in Our Local Parish

We went to Mass last night at the little mission church that is not too distant from our house. We love the pastor, who gives meaty homilies, and who is reverent (if not always completely liturgically correct) in his celebration of Mass. The church itself is the one I've mentioned where the sanctuary looks like a 1970's dining room, complete with a "captain's chair" for the priest and doilies on the end tables. Ugh.

BUT…

This week, at the end of Mass, Father invited everyone to sit down and said he wanted to make some corrections regarding the altar servers. Finally! An attempt to correct a minor liturgical abuse!

First, he backtracked and thanked them for be willing to serve. But then he told them that, since he usually closes his eyes when he prays the Our Father, he hadn't noticed that they were standing with their hands in the *"orans"* posture. (Under previous pastors, there was actually holding of hands by altar servers and priest as they stood behind the altar.)

Father made light of the correction by telling the servers that he was going to prepare them to serve in Rome. "If you go to Rome and you are a server," he said, "and you hold your arms out like that, the people watching on TV will be laughing at you!"

He then further instructed them to kneel before the altar during the Our Father, and to wait there to receive Holy Communion – in a kneeling position.

"You will be the example for the people," he told them – and in telling them, he was also teaching the congregation. "People are encouraged to kneel for Communion, and I will install a kneeler here for those who want to do that."

I was ready to applaud! But I refrained.

This is a small step, but I have hope! Father is a good, solid, fairly orthodox priest who has a sense of what the liturgy *should* be. He and I have talked about possible changes at this mission church before. He said the EF Mass for us (in a different church) for almost a year, and spoke to me a little bit about how it had changed him. We pray for another priest to be assigned to his parish so that he will be able to return to the celebration of the EF Mass; currently he is spread extremely thin.

Restoration of the Sacred at St. Peter's in Omaha, Nebraska

St. Peter's in Omaha, Nebraska, has received international attention for its efforts to restore the sacred via EWTN and StoryTel Foundation. The half-hour program which aired on EWTN in April 2013 is available on DVD, and it is much more than just a *glimmer* of hope! Just watching the video gave me a renewed sense of hope that such a restoration of the sacred can happen anywhere.

Here are some excerpts from a news article about the parish and the renewal going on there:

> "We're trying to do everything as faithfully as we can, as beautifully as we can, to what the Church has given us," Father Damien Cook, pastor of St. Peter Catholic Church in Omaha, Neb., told Catholic News Agency April 24.

> St. Peter's is "dedicated to the restoration of the sacred," he said, with Masses sung with Latin and chant, liturgies celebrated both facing the people and facing the altar, altar boys, Eucharistic adoration, evening prayer sung every day, processions and distribution of Communion at the altar rail.

"This is what we should do if we're going to be a fully faithful church according to Vatican II and the whole Tradition of the Church," said Father Cook.

. . .

Father Cook says he didn't come to St. Peter's with a program or plan to bring more people in. Instead, he asked the question of himself: "What do I think it means to be a priest and a pastor?"

Although this includes "all components of charity and catechesis," he said, "first and foremost, it has to start with the liturgy ... it's the source and summit. So the first thing that happened, that I could do, was liturgical formation."

The decisions Father Cook made "drew a lot of people back to the Church, which in turn re-vitalized our ministries, so now we've got all kinds of outpourings."

. . .

Father Cook believes beauty is particularly important in our age, because "we've lost so much in this very functional age, in terms of idolizing efficiency." He said the Gregorian chant sung at the parish transcends cultures and "brings people back to beauty."

Between the chanted Psalms at the Mass and the striking stained-glass windows made in Germany in the 1920s, at St. Peter's "everything goes together to make this beautiful symphony of truth, of goodness."

The adoption of chant has even affected the reverence of parishioners at St. Peter's. "I'm blessed with the congregation that comes," Father Cook said. "We have a lot of big families, in both the English- and Spanish-speaking communities, so they make noise, but I don't have to get up and remind them after Mass to be quiet."

"They stay in the pew for their thanksgiving and go outside to the vestibule to talk. And even the dress, what people wear, has really changed. Guests comment on how nicely people dress for Sunday Mass."

Father Cook reflected, "You never realize how much one person affects the person next to them, and we can bring each other down or really raise each other up," he said. "Even if we're not physically talking to someone, but just by what we wear and by deciding to stay after and pray at the altar rail or in our pew, it really reminds people. It really has helped here."[21]

The video says so much more than words can describe! Fr. Cook's comments are sincerely heart-felt; he comes across as a pastor dedicated to this renewal because he has seen what it has accomplished so far for his flock. This is truly a hope-filled DVD!

Insights of a Priest Attending Mass "Incognito"

Fr. Z ran a "guest post"[22] by a priest who attended a *Novus Ordo* Mass "incognito", in a way – for various reasons, he did not vest, nor attend in choir, but just went as a part of the congregation (Fr. Z's **emphases**):

For the first time in my eight years as a priest, I recently attended the holy Mass not as the presider, con-celebrant or while being vested in choir. The experience was quite

---

[21] http://www.ncregister.com/daily-news/new-film-depicts-dramatic-revival-of-omaha-parish#ixzz2Uzmr5OZS

[22] http://wdtprs.com/blog/2013/05/guest-post-a-priest-on-attending-a-novus-ordo-mass-in-the-congregation/

illuminating, for **it gave me insight to the regular obstacles many lay faithful face when attending Mass**. The experience, while insightful, was also **painful**. The occasion was the baccalaureate Mass for my youngest brother's graduation from high school. I purposely did not vest because I did not know what was in store, and I have a poor poker face when it comes to silly liturgy.

In all honesty, my attention was not to find any and all liturgical error or abuse, for I knew silliness was in store. That being said however, I quickly became aware of **how difficult it was to enter into this busy, disoriented, error filled liturgy**. Although this was a special Mass, I cannot say it was all that different from a typical Sunday Mass in my diocese. To be brief, it was **near impossible to wade through the obstacles in order to pray**, and the reason lay in three pieces: the music, the posture, and the manners of the ministers.

With regard to the reception of Holy Communion, he noticed this:

What I observed, as I exited the pew to let my family through, was a line similar to those at the entrance of a sporting event. Everyone was standing, and or talking, shuffling bit by bit to get to where they wanted to go, only to eventually sit down in padded pew comfort. They whole event was just like every other line they are daily in complete with background music and lines that move too slow. Again, it was **in no way effective in helping the faithful to move beyond themselves** into divine contemplation.

And he sums up his experience with this observation:

Let us face the facts. **We are celebrating the Mass like a protestant liturgy**, but we are doing it much poorer than most of them would ever dare to. If this is the environment we are constantly fostering to our faithful, it no wonder they are going somewhere else, or not at all. We are not proclaiming the truths of liturgy or fostering environments that point to these truths.

The "glimmer of hope" in this story is that this priest *noticed* that something was wrong with the way the *Novus Ordo* is typically celebrated in his diocese! Let us pray that his experience will shed some light on the subject for other priests as well. It's one thing to have the laity (at least a few of us) complaining about what's wrong with our liturgical celebrations; when a priest can see the situation from the layman's point of view, I think it is more likely that change will occur.

Section II:
The *Novus Ordo*

[In the older form of the Mass] there was an immediate tie-in with the synagogue, with the prayers at the foot of the altar. These were the psalms recited by the high priest as he would enter into the sanctuary. And of course, our faith is the fulfillment of the faith of the people of God from the time of the Old Covenant.

The prayers at the offertory are very rich in the 1962 Roman Missal. Those have been very much stripped down and actually changed in character in the missal of Pope Paul VI.

There was also a strong sense of our sinfulness and of the redemptive nature of the Holy Mass. Influenced, I believe by the times in which the reform was made, a lot of the language having to do with asking God's forgiveness and so forth was removed.

Raymond Cardinal Burke
in a Catholic News Agency video

Why I Dread Sunday Mass

To be fair, for almost a whole year, I did *not* dread Sunday Mass! That was because for almost a year, a priest in the parish 45 miles from our house celebrated Mass in the extraordinary form almost every Sunday. Now it's been weeks[23] since that priest has been able to celebrate that Mass, and that has left me and my husband with very few options, none of them good.

So, currently, I dread Sunday Mass.

We live in Eastern Oregon. The towns are far apart, and the Catholic churches even more widely spaced. But I'm not complaining about the distances; it's what's available (or not available) in each place that bothers me. And I'm not complaining about the lack of an extraordinary form Mass (okay, yes, I am complaining about that, but I am not opposed to attending a liturgically-correct, reverent *Novus Ordo* Mass as long as the rubrics are followed and the music is the official music of the Church. Did I hear someone say, "Yeah, good luck with *that*"?).

As soon as we knew it would be some weeks before we could attend "our" Mass, we debated the alternatives. We could go to the Cathedral on Sunday morning. On the plus side, this is the location closest to our home – 12 miles. In addition, it's a very beautiful, hundred-year-old church with lovely stained glass windows.

But...there is the music. Guitars. Tambourines. Ditties from *JourneySongs*. Additions like "Come Now, Children, Come" for the children's dismissal, and another tune for the sign of peace. I have spent the past year singing the Gregorian chant propers and ordinaries, in Latin, for the extraordinary form of the Mass. Nothing can compare to the beauty of those chants, as far as I'm concerned.

---

[23] Actually, now it's been years; it was "weeks" when I first wrote this article!

But surely there is something closer than the kindergarten songs that Oregon Catholic Press (OCP) has to offer in their various song books.

There is much more I object to at the Cathedral, but let's move on to the other options. We could attend the Sunday morning Mass at the same church in La Grande, 45 miles from home, where we've been attending the extraordinary form for the past year. But the same issue exists there: the music. OCP, this time *Breaking Bread*. Piano. Guitars. Tambourines. And occasionally, a trumpet. It's not worth the 90-minute round trip for that.

Okay...how about the little mission church? We attended there for a year or so, too, before we had access to the extraordinary form of the Mass. We were forewarned providentially, however, when a friend emailed me to say that she was in charge of the music there, and her strategy was to play CD's. Since there is a substantial Hispanic population, she would play two songs in English and two in Spanish. She said that the priest said most of the Mass in English and Spanish – that is, saying it in one language and then giving the translation in the other. He also gave the homily in both languages. This did not sound like something I wanted to endure.

We could go to the Saturday evening Mass at the Cathedral. That, actually, is the option we chose. There are musicians for that Mass every other week (and that's another story). On the off weeks, there are no musicians; the priest leads the singing, and it's all *a cappella*. I like hearing the people sing, though the choice of songs is not always (or even often) appropriate. It is the least offensive of our choices.

One week, when we just could not face another Mass with the priest at the Cathedral, we opted for the Saturday evening Mass in La Grande. It wasn't too bad, but...the music. Two women singing, with guitars. Standard OCP fare. Ugh.

I dread Sunday Mass. It's not just the music. It's what the music says about the state of our Church. Yes, I know Jesus is there. I try to focus on that fact, and on Him. But the music says that we don't truly understand the Mass. We don't get that it is an integrated whole, that it is meant to be sung, that it should all fit together, that it honors the King of the Universe.

I pray that we "get it" soon.

The New Translation is a Good Start, But...

I have no doubt that the new translation of the Roman Missal is a good thing. I've come to appreciate the Latin language and the way our Catholic identity and theology is wrapped up in the words of those prayers. A translation that is more faithful to the Latin and keeps Catholic theology in the forefront is most welcome.

The bottom line, though, in my humble opinion, is this: the new translation, *in and of itself*, is not enough to go very far in deepening our understanding of the Sacred Liturgy. Why? Well, for one thing, it's really a small matter for the laity to learn a few new responses at Mass; the bulk of the changes are in the prayers the priest prays. Now I could be way off the mark here, but I have a feeling that most people will *not* notice most of the changes in the priest's prayers. I'm not saying they don't pay attention, and I'm not saying that the words are not important: they are. I'm just saying that the changes will not make a huge impact on the laity, *unless there are other changes* in how the Mass is currently celebrated in most parishes.

In its promotion of the new translation on its website, the USCCB noted that (my **emphases**)

> [The Church] has been blessed with this opportunity to **deepen its understanding** of the Sacred Liturgy, and to appreciate its meaning and importance in our lives... [T]he parish community should be **catechized to receive the new translation**. Musicians and parishioners alike should soon be learning the various new and revised **musical settings** of the Order of Mass.

Some parishes prepared, and some didn't; some did a little, and some did a lot. But the above quote from the USCCB website hints at a very important component of the new translation which *could* make a big difference: "musical settings".

The third edition of the Roman Missal contains more music than the previous editions, and it reflects the Gregorian chant roots of the liturgy. There has been much talk (at least in some circles) of "singing the Mass" instead of simply "singing *at* Mass", and this is where the difference will be made, in my opinion. Singing the Mass – especially singing the Mass in the way it is presented in the new Roman Missal – is a much more far-reaching change than the changes in the translation. It's a change not just in the words, but in how the words are presented – with music that is truly liturgical.

Singing the Mass requires a priest to be willing to sing his parts; it requires the choir director to motivate the choir to learn a new style of singing along with some changes in the words; and it requires a congregation that will embrace the effort to learn new, sung, responses. None of this is easy, but it would be well worth it. It would raise the sense of awe and reverence in the liturgy by more than just a few notches. It would lead souls toward holiness.

I'm speaking here particularly about parishes like the ones I have access to, where guitars and tambourines abound, and Gregorian chant has been effectively banished. The preparation for the new translation in these parishes consisted of a few notices in the bulletin, and early distribution of pew cards with the new "people's responses" printed on them. There was no talk about new musical settings.

For some time now, the wonderful pipe organ in our Cathedral has stood silent, and the choir loft is empty because the "Folk Group" plays and sings from just off to the side of the sanctuary. In another parish near us, the choir loft is used, but the singers share the space with guitars, piano, trumpet, and tambourine – and sometimes a CD player. The liturgical music is from *JourneySongs* or *Breaking Bread*, and Latin is used very, very sparingly. The new translation is not going to overcome the overwhelming mediocrity and self-absorption conveyed by this type of music.

Other liturgical changes must be made if the new translation is to have a chance at deepening our understanding of and reverence for the Mass. The priest will have to stop taking the role of talk-show host. He will need to make sure that he absolutely "says the black and does the red" – that is, that he faithfully follows the rubrics and does not ad-lib. He will probably need to introduce the people to Mass being said *ad orientem*. To be truly faithful to Vatican II, the priest should lead his parish toward a greater appreciation of Latin. That's pretty easy to accomplish just by standardly singing the *Gloria*, the *Agnus Dei*, the *Sanctus*, *Pater Noster*, and even the *Credo* in Latin – the parts that we're supposed to know *as a minimum* according to Vatican II's *Sacrosanctum Concilium*.

Granted, the typical parish would probably not be able to handle all of these changes at once; but changes could be introduced gradually, with appropriate catechesis and preparation. My experience has been that choir people who are shown how a properly sung Mass all fits together become very excited about leaving their guitars and folk songs behind. If they are excited, they will infect the congregation.

All of this requires a pastor willing to implement these kinds of changes. But even more crucially importantly is a bishop willing to lead both the priests and the people in this direction, and to adequately support his priests who are working toward this goal. It's got to be a top-down effort: the bishop must encourage the priests, who must then lead the people into greater reverence for the liturgy. It can begin with the new translation, but it must not stop there…for the good of souls.

Save the liturgy, save the world.

The *Novus Ordo* Should Be Outgrown

The *Novus Ordo* Mass (the "New Mass") is something that can and should be outgrown. One wonders why the Church ever regressed into such a liturgy in the first place.

The *Novus Ordo* is, as Fr. Z has gently opined, the true "Mass for Children", while the Extraordinary Form is the true "Mass for Adults." The *Novus Ordo* can only take you so far. It may be capable of inspiring one to growth in the spiritual life, but it isn't capable of sustaining or developing spiritual maturity for the long haul. Once the limits are reached, there's no place else to go without abandoning the liturgical form from which all that is possible has been drunk.

The critical point beyond which it is impossible to grow without "changing forms" is the awareness that the Mass *is* the sacrifice of Calvary made present in an un-bloody form. A valid Mass in *any* form is always the sacrifice of Calvary, but that it's not really understood as such is evidenced by the way people (including the clergy) respond to this profound truth.

Is it really possible to imagine oneself at Calvary carrying on in the manner so typical of *Novus Ordo* Masses? The Protestant mentality has reduced the sacrifice to merely the "Lord's Supper", as if "Do this in memory of me" means "have dinner with each other and remember all I said and did". The "sign of peace" degenerates into a sappy "us"-focused exercise that interrupts the flow of a liturgy that is supposed to be God-focused. The homily is a nothing more than an email forward or a Face Book status that makes everyone feel warm and fuzzy, accepted and included.

To anyone with real spiritual maturity, Mass in a typical Catholic parish is embarrassing. And I think many people do have some spiritual maturity, and that deep down they know they should be embarrassed.

We're not at a petting zoo (despite the appearance of sheep and even poodles at Good Shepherd Sunday Masses; the donkey at Palm Sunday; and all the pets at the Sunday closest to the Feast of St Francis of Assisi). And we're not at a garden party with friends, at the "table of the Lord". We're at the *foot of the Cross*, and *Jesus is being offered in sacrifice.* Can we really see Our Blessed Mother hugging everyone, welcoming them to Calvary, and leading them in camp fire songs? "Thank you for coming! Hope you all had a good time! We *must* do this again! Maybe next week?"

Once this insight is grasped – the realization that *this is Calvary* – one has arrived at a point beyond which the *Novus Ordo* cannot go. All you can do is "change" the *Novus Ordo* to accommodate the growth of the faithful: you can begin to move towards the Latin version of the *Novus Ordo*; return to *ad orientem* worship; introduce the Gregorian chant propers. Once you've made these "changes", you arrive at a point that...well, the extraordinary form *already does this*, and its durability has proven itself for centuries.

One can, of course, *start* with the extraordinary form of the Mass, teaching it to children from the very beginning, as we see in EF Mass communities such as FSSP parishes. Children nurtured in this liturgical form and its spirituality *don't* outgrow it, and even at a young age know enough to be embarrassed when they are first exposed to the *Novus Ordo*. A friend whose children were raised on the EF Mass told me that she and her family had to attend a *Novus Ordo* Mass for some reason; afterwards, her children wanted to know whether that was really Catholic and whether they had really satisfied their Sunday obligation!

When I hear people rave about the *Novus Ordo* Mass and whine about how they just don't understand the Latin (look at the parallel English/Latin booklet for heaven's sake!), and Gregorian chant seems esoteric and too hard for anyone to sing (so *listen*), I want to say, "Someday I hope you respond to the grace of God and grow up, because that's what God is calling you to do. You can't be taken seriously as truly understanding what the Mass *is* and express yourself as you do. You're still an adolescent who believes that you're part of a whole generation with a new explanation. All generations think like that, until they grow up (if they do). You're at Calvary. Act like it."

The EF Mass has enough depth that one can never exhaust it. The *Novus Ordo*, by comparison, is childish and *demands* that one outgrow it if one aspires to spiritual maturity.

The evidence is in. The dots are able to be connected. We have *centuries* of evidence that the EF Mass "works", and the collapse of the *Novus Ordo* is inevitable. There's just no "there" there. The verdict is in. The liturgical experiment that is the *Novus Ordo* has failed spectacularly. Sure, there are communities here and there that are growing towards spiritual maturity *in spite of* the *Novus Ordo*, but, if they continue to grow, and if they finally see what the Mass *is*, they won't be able to continue as they are. The EF Mass is the only option left. For those who have already figured this out, why waste time treading water where they are?

How to Choose a New Parish

An email correspondent told me she and her family were moving to a new city, and asked for some advice on the task of choosing a new parish. Of course, I was more than happy to oblige.

When you're moving to a new town, of course you will seek to find the very best, most Catholic parish around! Well, at the very least, you'd like to avoid the happy/clappy liberal modernist ones. Wouldn't you? (If not, stop reading now, and find a different blog! Everything herein is my own ~~humble~~ opinion!)

On to the question: what can you do to optimize your search for a liturgically correct parish?

Hmm...you could call around to the various parishes within driving distance and ask how many women and girls wear chapel veils at Mass. If the receptionist says, "What's a chapel veil?", scratch that parish off your list. If the answer is, "Yeah, we have a few doily heads", harbor grave reservations. Unfortunately, these are the most likely responses.

You could just look at the parish Mass schedule, too. See if they have an EF Mass, or a NO Mass in Latin – anything that sounds vaguely traditional; it does happen occasionally! If they have a Life Teen Mass, I'd have to give the parish a thumbs-down. A "charismatic" Mass is also a warning sign. Of course, it is possible that a parish might offer the whole gamut...depends on the size of the community you're investigating. And I do know of a parish that offers *both* an EF Mass *and* a Life Teen Mass. Go figure.

And do they regularly offer a Communion Service or two during the week? Uh oh. Either there's a lazy pastor who doesn't value his gift and responsibility of saying Mass every day, or you've got some heavy-hitters among the laity who have hijacked the Sacred Liturgy so that they can be almost-priests. This is especially common among ex-nuns.

Another thought: Look at the parish web page. Do they actually have a photo of the pastor? Is he called Reverend John McPriest, or listed simply as "Father John"? (And is he wearing his collar, or just a polo shirt?) Do they list deacons as Rev. Mr. James Dalmatic, or do they just mention Deacon Tom and Deacon Bob? If they list a Deacon Shirley, you're in trouble.

The parish's on-line bulletin also offers some clues. Take a look and see what kind of activities they offer. If they feature their Respect Life group front and center, you might just have a winner! On the other hand, if they have a "Centering Prayer" group and lots of "Justice and Peace", but *no* Respect Life group, look for another parish! Quick!

Mission statements…yes, every parish seems to have one. Sometimes I wonder why. They all tend to sound the same while trying to sound just a little different. But don't we all have the same mission? "Go, therefore, and make disciples of all nations, baptizing them in the name of the Father, and of the Son, and of the holy Spirit, teaching them to observe all that I have commanded you" (Matthew 28:19-20). Well, some of those "mission statements" we see on websites and parish bulletins are quite telling…and usually not in a good way. For instance:

> St. Andrew is a faith community baptized into one body, which honors and celebrates diversity. We welcome and include persons of every color, language, ethnicity, origin, ability, sexual orientation, gender expression, marital status, and life situation.[24]

Obviously, it is not wrong to *welcome* all of those different people. "Include" is a loaded word, though. Do they "include" all in terms of receiving Holy Communion, regardless of their "life situation" (e.g., open homosexual lifestyle, divorced-with-live-in-sexual-partner, etc.) and state of grace (or lack thereof)? The parish from whose website I copied the above mission statement also sports a photo of a group of their parishioners participating in the local "Gay Pride" parade a few years ago.

Here's another mission statement:

> We, St. Mary's Parish, are a people responding to Christ's call to conversion, new life and discipleship with a nurturing Community.
>
> We celebrate this new life in Scripture and the Sacraments of the Roman Catholic tradition.
>
> Our Celebration impels and transforms us to be Spirit filled individuals who can reach out and minister to all people challenging and enabling them to build God's Kingdom of justice and holiness.

Loaded terms: "Spirit-filled" and "justice". That's sad to say, but it's true. Seems to me that oftentimes the people using the term "Spirit-filled" mean something along the lines of "I have the Holy Spirit guiding me; I don't need the Magisterium of the Church". And "justice"…ah yes, justice. Of course, as Catholics we are all for "justice". But unfortunately, too many of the people promoting "justice" are likely just promoting "gay rights" or even "women's reproductive choice" (they don't like the word "abortion").

---

[24] http://www.standrewchurch.com/

As an aside, here's a great quote from Pope Benedict XVI on the meaning of "justice and peace":

> Justice is not a mere human convention. When, in the name of supposed justice, the criteria of utility, profit, and material possession come to dominate, the value and dignity of human beings can be trampled underfoot. Justice is a virtue which guides the human will, prompting us to give others what is due to them by reason of their existence and their actions. Likewise, peace is not the mere absence of war, or the result of man's actions to avoid conflict; it is, above all, a gift of God which must be implored with faith, and which has the way to its fulfillment in Jesus. True peace must be constructed day after day with compassion, solidarity, fraternity, and collaboration on everyone's part.[25]

There are other loaded words to watch for in parish bulletins. Here's a bulletin blurb about a catechetical program a parish was promoting. See if you can spot the warning sign:

> Here's a sample schedule for Sunday mornings.
> 9:40 – meet in *Gathering Space* for Coffee & donuts & overview of the day's topic
> 10:00 – break up into groups for families, adults, teens. Folks in these groups will do a variety of activities and some additional catechesis. We even have a Veggie Tales group for younger children.
> 10:45 – come back to the *Gathering Space* for a closing prayer service and announcements.

---

[25] http://www.catholicculture.org/news/headlines/index.cfm?storyid=12966

Aha! I thought you might see it! "Gathering Space"? Hmm. I dunno. Could mean nothing. Then again…well, I'm just sayin'.

Finally, of course, visit the church. If you see felt banners for First Communion, you're probably in 90% of the parishes in the US, but that's not necessarily a good thing. Where is it written that First Communion must be accompanied by a felt banner with the child's name on it? Also, if you see sweeping streamers of gauze-y fabric…run for your life!

Mass, My Cry of Anguish, and the Year of Faith

For me, Sundays are…Just. Not. Good. I know, I've said that before. But now I have progressed to a new level of anguish.

It's not that we have more egregious liturgical abuses than other parishes do. It could be a lot worse. Still, the bad music, the ad-libbed prayers, the often-ridiculous "prayers of the faithful", the glad-handing and racing around the church at the "sign of peace", and so on…*ad nauseam*…constitutes a continuous grating on the nerves.

But now the problem is that I am becoming more and more aware of the *theological* issues with the *Novus Ordo* Mass. I can't ignore it any longer. I can't pretend. I know too much.

On the Sundays when we attend Mass celebrated by a fairly orthodox priest, I get my hopes up a little, and I think, "Maybe this week I can hang onto my state of grace long enough to receive Holy Communion"…because usually I don't. Recently, though, even when I have been able to overlook the bad music and a few liturgical abuses, I cannot bring myself to receive.

That's because, on the heels of that thought about receiving Holy Communion, I wonder how I can receive at a Mass that seems to be a little confused in its own perception of itself, so to speak. It's a Mass that says it's Catholic, but wants very badly to be Protestant. It fools most of the people most of the time. But it seems to me that it can't fool the people who have attended and plumbed the depths of the ancient Rite, the Mass of the Ages, the "extraordinary form" of the Mass, the Traditional Latin Mass, the Tridentine Mass…whatever you want to call it. In my own mind, I often call it "the *real* Mass". (And yes, I know the NO is a valid Mass, assuming the basic conditions are met.)

What are the ways in which the NO Mass loses touch with theological reality? Let me count the ways…or just a few of them.

First, there is the problem of the NO Mass seeing itself as an "assembly" rather than a "sacrifice". It's a "memorial of the Lord's Supper" rather than the sacrifice of the Cross. Its essence is defined as the "gathering" of the People of God". When I was the secretary at my parish, it was my duty to prepare a little script each week for the "announcer" to read, giving a little summary of the Gospel, etc. I always included the line, "Now let us take a few minutes of silence to prepare ourselves for the Holy Sacrifice of the Mass." One announcer would *never* say the word "sacrifice"; he said "celebration". (And most announcers could not remain silent for more than 30 seconds before saying, "Now let us stand for our opening song.")

Second, there's the problem of the role of the priest. In the EF Mass, you can see that the priest is *really* a priest, and that he offers the sacrifice for us, and that it is a Really Important Event. The NO Mass is defined by the *GIRM* as "the People of God…called together, with a priest presiding and acting in the person of Christ" (§27). The important thing to note is that the NO revisers made the priest a "presider", and out of that he has become a talk-show host. In the EF Mass, the introit is a time of the priest's preparation for the Mass. In the NO, we've lost (or displaced) the prayers at the foot of the altar[26], and the introit is now the "entrance hymn" – just a parade up to the sanctuary where the priest opens with a funny comment to break the ice.

Does it *have* to be this way? No. Does the theology of the New Mass expose itself to this with great abandon? Yes.

---

[26]The Confiteor and absolution in the EF have become the Penitential Rite in the OF; and, whereas in the EF only the priest and ministers pray these prayers – sotto voce – in the OF everyone prays them – aloud. The psalm, some of the prayers, and versicles and responses were omitted in the OF.

Third, the "new translation" notwithstanding, we still have weak prayers. "Sin" has been put back into them in places, but they still lack the force, the power, the no-nonsense-tell-it-like-it character of the *real* prayers. Just look at a 1962 Missal to see the difference. The handful of uninitiated people to whom I have shown those prayers have all expressed astonishment at the unabashed beauty and reverence of those prayers.

Fourth, the concept of the Real Presence of Jesus in the Eucharist has been diluted and distorted, so that it's no wonder people don't really believe in the Real Presence any more. The *GIRM* states that "Christ is really present in the very liturgical assembly gathered in his name, in the person of the minister, in his word, and indeed substantially and continuously under the Eucharistic species." Now, all of those things may be true, but lumping it all together that way, brings the Real Presence down a few notches, to say the least, and fails to show with *actions* the ineffable and sublime meaning of the *real* Real Presence.

In addition, the omission of *actions* that show the greater reverence due the Real Presence, have led people away from the sense of awe we should experience when we are in that Presence, and when we receive Holy Communion. Reception of Communion standing and in the hand, the disparaging of veils for women, the casual dress permitted for lay ministers…these are all answers to the question, "Why don't people believe in the Real Presence?"

What makes me really sad – and really angry – is that so much of this appears to have been done on purpose by those with a modernist view and agenda at the Second Vatican Council. They *purposely* Protestantized the Mass. The evidence is out there; there are many accounts of what was said behind the scenes, what the modernists wanted to accomplish, the involvement of Protestants in guiding the "reform" of the Mass. (See for instance, Romano Amerio's *Iota*

Unum, Anne Muggeridge's *Desolate City*, and titles like *Liturgical Shipwreck* by Michael Davies.)

The saddest fact of all is that most people aren't really conscious of any of this. Some people seem to suspect that the Mass has been "Protestantized" but don't know how to articulate it any further than that. Others don't even think about it. It's Mass…that's all…it's just Mass. "We've always done it this way," they say. When something goes really crazy – like a clown Mass, for instance – they might object…or they might think, "Hey, *that* was a fun variation on a theme!"

Yet, the theological problems *do* manifest themselves in our lives. *Lex orandi, lex credendi:* The underlying theology of the Mass *does* affect our sense of Catholic identity, our knowledge of our faith, and our ability – and even our motivation – to effectively evangelize others (even our own children!).

The faithful who understand the problem are labeled "traditionalist", at best. They are often outcasts in their own parish. Their concerns about liturgical abuses are dismissed as "overly scrupulous". They are the only women wearing veils at Mass. They are the ones plugging their ears against the guitars and tambourines. They are the ones mourning in the pews at the sight of people texting while in line to receive Holy Communion. They are the ones who drive hours one-way to attend a Traditional Latin Mass, even if that Mass is said in an SSPX chapel *(gasp!)*.

On October 11, 2012, the Church entered into a "Year of Faith" proclaimed by Pope Benedict XVI. We're encouraged to study the documents of Vatican II and the *Catechism of the Catholic Church*. Will studying the documents of Vatican II change things? I suppose it could…if the people who study them are willing to actually *see* that Gregorian chant is to be given first place, that Latin was never meant to be abandoned, and that it was never mandated that the priest face the people during Mass. Etc.

Call me a skeptic, but I just don't see that happening. And even if it did – which could certainly result in some improvements – we would still have the problem of the insidious creeping modernism inherent in the Vatican II documents, and which also can be found in the *Catechism of the Catholic Church.* How does faith grow in that kind of poisoned ground?

In *Porta Fidei*[27], the document introducing the Year of Faith, Pope Benedict XVI quotes Blessed John Paul II, who said that the Vatican II texts:

> ... *"have lost nothing of their value or brilliance.* They need to be **read correctly**, to be widely known and taken to heart as important and normative texts of the Magisterium, within the Church's Tradition ... I feel more than ever in duty bound to point to the Council as *the great grace bestowed on the Church in the twentieth century:* there we find a sure compass by which to take our bearings in the century now beginning." (*italics* in original; my **emphases**)

The Holy Father adds:

> I would also like to emphasize strongly what I had occasion to say concerning the Council a few months after my election as Successor of Peter: "if we **interpret** and **implement** it guided by a **right hermeneutic**, it can be and can become increasingly powerful for the **ever necessary renewal** of the Church."

---

[27]http://www.vatican.va/holy_father/benedict_xvi/motu_proprio/documents/hf_ben-xvi_motu-proprio_20111011_porta-fidei_en.html

Well…there's the rub. The Council has been "interpreted" to distraction over the last 50 years, giving us the "Spirit of Vaddican Too" which haunts many now-closed parishes. The fact that so much interpretation has been necessary in the first place ought to give us pause. That "interpretation" gave us the *Novus Ordo* Mass, after all.

With all due respect to the Holy Father, I think that it's time to admit that there might be at least the shadow of an "elephant in the living room" in the sense that modernistic elements may have crept into the Vatican II documents. Until we examine the ways in which the ambiguous wording[28] of some of the Council's documents may have damaged the Church in the last 50 years, we aren't going to make much progress in a "new evangelization".

If that's a "downer", so be it. A Pollyanna attitude and rose-colored glasses will not re-fill the pews or the seminaries. Neither will it increase our faith.

At least, that's how I see it.

---

[28] "In many places, [the Council Fathers] had to find **compromise formulas**, in which, often, the positions of the majority are located immediately next to those of the minority, designed to delimit them. Thus, **the conciliar texts themselves have a huge potential for conflict**, open the door to a **selective reception** in either direction." - Cardinal Walter Kasper, L'Osservatore Romano, April 12, 2013

Glimmers of Hope, Part 2

"Where Can We Go for the Older Form?"

At our local mission parish, we are praying the Rosary on Tuesday nights, for the healing of the ills within the Church and our nation. Well, at least two of us are! At the end of the Rosary, I asked the other woman if she knew the Salve Regina. She indicated that she did...sort of...and it was in "the book", so we sang it together. Then she pointed to the next song - it was the Ave Maria - and said, "How about this one?" So I sang, and she followed. Then we did one verse of *O Sanctissima*. She had no problem trying to sing the Latin.

We talked briefly about music in the Mass, and about the older form of the Mass. I explained about *ad orientem* worship, and she was nodding and saying, "Oh yes, that makes sense", etc. I asked her if she'd ever attended an EF Mass, and she shook her head.

She paused for a moment, considering that thought with furrowed brow, and then asked, "Where can we go to attend the older form?"

The ol' $64,000 question!

You see, many people do not know the riches of the EF Mass. They have not a clue what they're missing! They won't ask the local pastor to provide it, because they don't even know it's their right (and their RITE!!).

In other words, the faithful don't know their faith; they are ignorant of their heritage. And it's not their fault, really. Priests and bishops who *do* know this heritage have not shared it, and some have even tried to hide it.

But word is getting out anyway! Some people who have no experience of the "Old Mass", and no "baggage" to inhibit their spiritual desires, are beginning to wonder, and beginning to seek access to the extraordinary form. This can only be a good thing!

Hope Springs Eternal in Eastern Oregon

Hoping for the best, but expecting the mediocre, I went to Sunday morning Mass in La Grande, Oregon, at Our Lady of the Valley.

The drawing card was the fact that our new Bishop Liam Cary was scheduled to say Mass there and administer the sacrament of Confirmation. There were also a number of children receiving First Holy Communion, though I wasn't aware of that when I planned to make the 90-minute round trip to La Grande.

I wanted to see Bishop Cary "in action", and I wanted to see what the parish would do in terms of liturgy suited to a bishop.

I've been to Mass at Our Lady of the Valley plenty of times; we attended there on a weekly basis for almost a year. I knew what the choir was capable of, and I knew what they usually do. My hopes were, sadly, not very high.

But I was surprised. The music, sung by the main choir joined by some of the outlying mission musicians, included a Gregorian chant ordinary (*Kyrie, Gloria, Sanctus*, and *Agnus Dei*). There were a couple of traditional hymns which sounded nice, although if that darn piano could be transformed into an organ, it would've been much better! There were a couple of standard OCP ditties…but Rome was not built in a day.

Our Lady of the Valley does not have a deacon, but there is an ordained permanent deacon at one of the missions, and he served today. OLV's instituted acolyte – a very capable and reverent server – was on hand as well, joined by one of the diocese's seminarians who lives in La Grande. I believe there were a couple of altar boys serving as miter and crosier bearers, but unfortunately there were also a couple of very cute little girls bouncing around (almost literally) the sanctuary. Again, Rome wasn't built in a day!

Bishop Cary had a wonderful episcopal presence! His homily was geared somewhat to the young confirmands and first communicants, but it was certainly not juvenile. He talked about some "wonderful-sounding words" - like "transubstantiation" and "epiclesis"! He was gracious and pastoral throughout.

And Bishop Cary can sing the Mass! How amazing, in Eastern Oregon, to have a correctly and beautifully chanted Preface followed by a fitting *Sanctus*! There were no tambourines, and the trumpet was silent, as the chanting voices of the little schola floated down from the choir loft.

The First Communicants were all given First Holy Communion on the tongue (and by intinction as well) – something I've never witnessed at a First Communion Mass in this diocese! The Confirmands were given the choice as to how to receive, and I only noticed one young person receiving on the tongue.

"Cute" did make its appearance, however, as the First Communicants were gathered in front of the altar after Communion to sing "Oh, How I Love Jesus". Yes, it was cute – *very, very cute*. And then the whole congregation was cleverly led into joining them for the last rousing chorus, and after that everyone applauded loudly. The trump card was played, but at least it wasn't at the *beginning* of Communion. There was more applause as the pastor thanked everyone involved.

Still, if we could go back and edit out everything from the last person receiving Holy Communion up to the Bishop giving the final blessing, it would have been a pretty good liturgy.

And even with the "cute" card, and that trumpet (which was played during a couple of songs), and way too much applause, I still give the Mass a "thumbs up", considering that it was far above the standard for the Masses I've experienced in Eastern Oregon.

After Mass, Bishop Cary stood on the steps of the church and greeted every single person who presented himself to be greeted. He did that with patience and attention, without seeming hurried or tired or overwhelmed. He exuded grace, confidence, gentleness, and interest in each person.

Let us pray that the Holy Spirit moves Bishop Cary to move the celebration of the Mass in an ever more reverent direction! And let us also pray that he defend and even promote the celebration of the extraordinary form of the Mass.

Section III:

The Music at Mass

All other things being equal, Gregorian chant holds pride of place because it is proper to the Roman Liturgy. Other types of sacred music, in particular polyphony, are in no way excluded, provided that they correspond to the spirit of the liturgical action and that they foster the participation of all the faithful.

Since faithful from different countries come together ever more frequently, it is fitting that they know how to sing together at least some parts of the Ordinary of the Mass in Latin, especially the Creed and the Lord's Prayer, set to the simpler melodies.

General Instruction of the Roman Missal, §41

Musical Memory Lane

I have some memories about coming into the Church that have to do with music.

First, I remember thinking that Catholic music was particularly bad. Of course, I was comparing it to the "contemporary Christian" music which was played at the Pentecostal services I attended. The music there was better, I thought, precisely *because* it was contemporary; it was "relevant". It also had a beat, and you could dance to it, which we did. :-/ Oh my!

Back in those RCIA days, I asserted that I was going to maintain "dual citizenship" because I wanted to go to the Pentecostal assembly – for the music. I only went back once, though; learning about the Real Presence of Jesus in the Eucharist made me acutely aware that, despite what I felt about the music, something was certainly missing at the Pentecostal church.

Second, I remember when the season of Lent began, and the "adult choir" (as opposed to the "folk group") at our parish sang the *Agnus Dei*. In Latin. Gregorian chant. I had not a clue what was going on; it was so far removed from what we'd been singing that I turned to my husband and asked him what it was. It was *different*, I thought, in a good way.

The third memory is from the second Easter vigil I attended – the one-year anniversary of my having been received into the Church. We had moved from California to Baker City, Oregon in that year, and I was experiencing the Easter vigil at the Cathedral. It happened that a certain monk also attended. I have written of it elsewhere:

> As Mass began, I spotted a tall, hooded figure in the procession. Turning to my cradle-Catholic husband, I asked, "What is *that*?" This was also my first introduction to

Gregorian chant: The Monk sang the *Exultet*. I didn't know what I was hearing, but I knew it that it was ancient and sacred, and it evoked in me a new depth of longing for God[29].

He didn't even sing it in Latin. But I thought it was the most beautiful thing I'd ever heard.

Recently, I read the full text of Msgr. Andrew Wadsworth's speech at the 2010 Southeastern Liturgical Music Symposium, August 21, 2010. It's well worth reading in its entirety; here are some of his comments (my **emphases**):

> ...I am sure that many of you here today were among the first to recognize **that a change of translation, a change which implies a difference of style, register and content, would have considerable implications for our liturgical music.** I am sure it will have occurred to you that it would not just be a matter of **adapting our current settings and songs to the new texts**, rather in the way that one might alter an old and well-loved garment to meet the demands of an increasing or decreasing waist-line! But rather, the new texts would quite naturally inspire new music which responds more directly to the character of the texts themselves, reflecting in an original way their patterns of accentuation, their cadence and their phrasing. Is it too much to hope that this might be a wonderful opportunity for **reassessing the current repertoire of liturgical music in the light of our rich musical patrimony** and like the good housekeeper being able to bring out of the store **treasures both new and old**?[30]

Unfortunately, I am seeing in our diocese a tendency to want to do just exactly what Msgr. Wadsworth suggests is a mistake: adapting current musical settings to the new texts. The new translation – the

---

[29] From "My Favorite Priest", *Homiletic and Pastoral Review,* May 2007
[30] http://www.chantcafe.com/p/towards-future-singing-mass-by-msgr.html

third edition of the *Roman Missal* – contains more music than any previous edition. And folks, it is *not* music by Marty Haugen and Bob Hurd! And we *do* have a "rich musical patrimony" to draw from, but it is *not* meant to be accompanied by guitars, tambourines, and/or saxophones. It is Gregorian chant. In the new Missal, it is Gregorian chant in both Latin and English; it is simplified and certainly sing-able (and will make you thirst for the authentic Latin stuff!). It makes sense in the context of the Mass itself. What a concept!

Having attended a workshop which utilized some materials from the Liturgical Institute's *Mystical Body, Mystical Voice* program[31], I understand exactly what Msgr. Wadsworth is saying in this next paragraph:

> Maybe the greatest challenge that lies before us is the invitation once again to **sing the Mass rather than merely to sing at Mass**. This echoes the injunctions of the Council Fathers in the Constitution on the Sacred Liturgy and reflects our deeply held instinct that the majority of the texts contained in the Missal can and in many cases should be sung. This means not only the congregational acclamations of the Order of Mass, but also the orations, the chants in response to the readings, the Eucharistic prayer and the antiphons which accompany the Entrance, the Offertory and the Communion processions. **These proper texts are usually replaced by hymns or songs that have little relationship to the texts proposed by the Missal or the Graduale Romanum and as such a whole element of the liturgy of the day is lost or consigned to oblivion.** For the most part, they exist only as spoken texts. We are much the poorer for this, as these texts (which are often either Scriptural or a gloss on the Biblical text) represent the

---

[31] http://www.mbmv.org/

Church's own reading and meditation on the Scriptures. **As chants, they are a sort of musical lectio divina** pointing us towards the riches expressed in that day's liturgy. For this reason, I believe that it is **seriously deficient** to consider that planning music for the liturgy ever begins with a blank sheet: **there are texts given for every Mass in the Missal and these texts are intended for singing**.

In the workshop I attended, participants were reminded of the rich Catholic heritage that lies beneath the surface of the Liturgy, building on almost 2000 years of Christianity as well as several thousand years more of our roots in Judaism. The Mass is more than it appears on the surface, and participants were led into a renewal of their understanding of the liturgy's spiritual depths and its true meaning. Instruction in singing the Mass was also included, making use of all that music in the new edition. This highlighted the fact that the USCCB is encouraging priests and the faithful to reclaim some of the lost traditions of the Church by singing the Mass from start to finish.

So…from my scattered memories of my initial Catholic music experience, coupled with my experience with chant over the last few years, and joining that to the potential of the new translation, I must simply urge you:

Go! Run – do not walk! – to the nearest "*Mystical Body, Mystical Voice*" workshop (or use the on-line resources)! But *sing the Mass*!

Sacred Music and Catholic Identity

A Protestant Face Book friend – addressing her mostly Protestant friends – posted this "status":

Just wondering, when worshipping in a corporate setting, where is the line between letting go and worshipping freely, and self-indulgence that causes distraction and becomes a stumbling block?

Ah, yes. I was a Pentecostal Christian for a number of years. The music was important. The music was uplifting. As I was being drawn to the Catholic Church, I still held out for the music – with electric guitars, drums, keyboard – of the Pentecostal church I attended. The music at the Catholic church – with acoustic guitars, drums, and piano – sucked. I said I'd go to Mass to receive Jesus, but I'd still go to the Pentecostal church for the music…but only as long as I was enjoying the music, of course.

At some point, I came to wonder if we were worshiping the music instead of the Lord.

"Letting go and worshipping freely" in the sense my Face Book friend is using that phrase, is, I believe, something you do in the privacy of your own room. Public worship – liturgy – is not the place for individualized expressions of praise. It's not the place for debates within the music ministry about which hymns or songs to sing.

And that is why *liturgical* worship is so liberating.

Well…let me qualify that: I'm talking about liturgical worship that follows the rubrics, and liturgical music that follows the mind of the Church rather than the mind of the choir director or the liturgy committee or the "worship team". I'm talking about *sacred* music.

The liturgy mandated by the Church takes away the petty arguments about style and "substance". Gregorian chant has pride of place; the proper chants of the Mass are determined from ages ago and have evolved out of the wisdom of the Church. The liturgy becomes what it is meant to be – a public expression of worship – by unifying all of the faithful as they use the same words and worship in a *universal* way.

The definition of sacred or religious music depends explicitly on the original intended use of the musical pieces or songs; that is to say, sacred music is **music which was composed for the Liturgy**. In 1967, the document *Musicam Sacram (Instruction on Music in the Liturgy)* was promulgates specifically to direct the choice of liturgical music within the context of the changes in the Mass brought about by Vatican II; it says:

4. It is to be hoped that pastors of souls, musicians and the faithful will gladly accept these norms and put them into practice, uniting their efforts to attain the true purpose of sacred music, "which is the glory of God and the sanctification of the faithful."

(a) By sacred music is understood that which, being created for the celebration of divine worship, is endowed with a certain holy sincerity of form.

(b) The following come under the title of sacred music here: Gregorian chant, sacred polyphony in its various forms both ancient and modern, sacred music for the organ and other approved instruments, and sacred popular music, be it liturgical or simply religious.

The distinction between "sacred" music and "religious" music and the criteria for determining to what "degree" a particular composition approaches the adjective "sacred" dates back to Pope St Pius X's 1903 Motu proprio *Inter sollicitudines* (a.k.a., *Tra le sollecitudini*)). It is significant that this distinction has been repeated in every papal document on sacred music since then, even until our own days.

So where's the freedom then? Well, the freedom is in following the mind of the Church. Non-Catholic Christians can generally agree that following Jesus is liberating – there is absolute freedom in following Truth. Non-Christians will argue that Christianity puts all kinds of constraints on human behavior, so we are not "free". They don't understand that we are bound by sin when we follow our own fallen, sinful nature.

In the same way, our fallen human nature makes itself known in the "freedom" of style of worship in non-Catholic Christian services. My Face Book friend mentions the fine line between "letting go and worshipping freely" and "self-indulgence that causes distraction". Been there, done that! When there are no rules, human concupiscence can run wild, and individuals can justify their behavior on the grounds that "the Spirit led me" – even, and maybe especially, in the context of the very worship of God. We end up having music for its entertainment value, and when you do that, you have debates, because not everyone is "entertained" in the same way by particular types of music.

The Mass, though – especially the "old" Mass, the "traditional Latin Mass", the "extraordinary form" of the Mass – allows for "*actual*" participation of the faithful. That participation is *first* internal, in the depths of one's soul, rather than in the external manifestation of singing, dancing, waving of hands, falling to the floor, etc.[32] The priest leads us in prayer to God, and we are united behind him. The music – Gregorian chant in particular – carries our minds upward to God, rather than centering our thoughts on ourselves. Truly liturgical, sacred music does not mimic the popular music of the

---

[32] Actually it's not an "either/or", but – in typical Roman thought – "both/and": i.e., *partipatio actuosa* must *first* be interior, and *then* secondly exterior (e.g., responding to the dialog, posture, procession)

time. It must itself be timeless, objectively beautiful, and "traditional" rather than "contemporary". Contemporary quickly becomes trite.

I suspect that if Protestant musicians began to use Catholic sacred music – such as Gregorian chant and sacred polyphony, which are all based on the Psalms – their services would become much more Catholic. And sadly, when Catholic musicians insist on "contemporary Christian" music for Mass, the Mass begins to resemble a Protestant service.

Our sacred music is a source of our Catholic identity. It's worth hanging on to…or, in most parishes, re-introducing.

What Happened to Singing the Mass?

Wendi, a blogger in the mid-West, wrote about a trip her family made to the Cathedral of their diocese (my **emphases**):

> So we took the opportunity to go to Mass at the Cathedral. It's the first time we've done so since moving to this diocese.
>
> Mass was...interesting. The music was ok, but actually a little disappointing. What they did sing was beautiful, although the choir was sometimes overpowered by the organ.
> I just **expected them to sing...more**. It was the 11:00 Mass. It was the Cathedral...you know the Bishop's home parish. So I expected that all the first degree stuff would be sung...it wasn't.
>
> As I said, a little disappointing.
>
> I thought the whole **point of being the Bishop was leading by example**. So...it then follows that his home parish should do that too...right? I could have gone to the same Mass in **any Suburban parish** and it would have been **pretty much the same**.
>
> Ah well...it did give me a greater appreciation for what I have at home.[33]

I admit I do not have the opportunity (or inclination) to travel far and wide – even in my own diocese – to see whether the new translation of the Roman Missal has resulted in an improvement in the music, and whether or not priests are singing their parts of the Mass. But I suspect that what a correspondent wrote to me is true:

---

[33] http://cradlestories.blogspot.com/2012/04/trip-to-cathedral.html

...[There has been a] consummate failure from the top down to properly implement the new English translation of the *Missale Romanum*. The Church clearly intends that the Mass (yes, the *Novus Ordo Missae*) be *sung*: that's patently obvious from the profusion of chant settings for the Order of Mass – something unprecedented in comparison to the edition that's been in use in the US now since the seventies.

The new missal provides either the chant or the chant formulae for singing the entire Mass – Propers, Ordinary, and Order of Mass. There's no excuse now to NOT sing the Mass.

Prior to the implementation of the new translation, the USCCB's website promotion of the changes stated (my **emphases**):

[The Church] has been blessed with this opportunity to **deepen its understanding** of the Sacred Liturgy, and to appreciate its meaning and importance in our lives... [T]he parish community should be **catechized to receive the new translation**. Musicians and parishioners alike should soon be learning the various new and revised **musical settings** of the Order of Mass.

Some parishes prepared, and some didn't; some did a little, and some did a lot.

But the above quote from the USCCB website hints at a very important component of the new translation which *could* have made a big difference: "musical settings".

The third edition of the Roman Missal contains more music than the previous editions, and it reflects the Gregorian chant roots of the liturgy. There has been much talk (at least in some circles) of "singing the Mass" instead of simply "singing *at* Mass". Singing the Mass – especially singing the Mass in the way it is presented in the new Roman Missal – is a much more far-reaching change than the changes in the translation. It's a change not just in the words, but in how the words are presented – with music that is truly liturgical.

Singing the Mass requires a priest to be willing to sing his parts; it requires the choir director to motivate the choir to learn a new style of singing along with some changes in the words; and it requires a congregation that will embrace the effort to learn new, sung, responses. None of this is easy, but it would be well worth it. It would bring up the sense of awe and reverence in the liturgy by more than just a few notches. It would lead souls toward holiness.

But it also requires a bishop who will lead his priests in implementing the singing of the Mass.

Bishop Olmsted of the Diocese of Phoenix is the only bishop I know of who has done some serious teaching about singing the Mass. That doesn't mean others haven't, but Bishop Olmsted's teaching was highly visible; he published his comments in his monthly column in the *Catholic Sun*, the diocesan newspaper, as a four-part series[34].I don't know whether the Mass is sung at Bishop Olmsted's cathedral, but at least the priests of the diocese – as well as the faithful – should have a pretty good idea what Bishop Olmsted thinks about the importance of liturgical music. [*When this post was written, then Bishop Alexander Sample of the Diocese of Marquette had not yet promulgated his pastoral letter on sacred music.*]

I did notice, as I was researching this topic, that Bishop Joseph B. McFadden of the Diocese of Harrisburg, PA, instituted a diocesan-wide program for "singing the Mass", complete with a "liturgical musicians symposium" in 2011. Perhaps such preparation and promotion of singing the Mass is more common than I have been thinking. Let's hope so!

---

[34] You can search the archives for Bishop Olmstead's series at http://www.catholicsun.org/category/views/bishop-olmsted/

Meanwhile, where I live, there hasn't been much change in the music at our local cathedral, nor at the surrounding parishes. There is a new *Gloria*, of course, but the choir chose a setting with a repeating refrain, which is clearly not permitted (*GIRM* §53). At the diocesan level, a rather bland and notably music-less presentation was created and is available at the diocesan website for parishes to show as a Power Point presentation, or simply download a booklet. But the presentation merely introduces the changes in the people's parts, and "singing the Mass" isn't even mentioned.

My general sense is that, in most parishes across the country, few have switched to singing the chants, even in English, and priests don't seem to be using their singing voices.

That is a problem which those of us in the pews can't fix. Those who have been exposed to the beauty of the chant begin to see how the liturgy can become an integrated whole rather than a hodge-podge of styles and languages. But they also immediately see that the priest needs to sing his parts, too, and they ask, "How can we get Father to sing the prayers?"

The answer is: we can't.

That's where the leadership of the bishop comes in, which brings us back to the point Wendi made in her post: bishops should be leading by example. When they do, we'll see the Mass begin to be sung.

And *then* we will begin to see progress in returning the liturgy to its rightful state of beauty and noble simplicity.

As for helping the faithful learn more about chant, and helping priests to learn how to sing their parts, the Church Music Association of America (CMAA) does so admirably by conducting an annual colloquium[35]. In 2012, the Reverend Robert Pasley, CMAA's

---

[35] http://musicasacra.com/colloquium

chaplain, issued a special invitation to priests to the event, noting (my **emphases**):

> ...Pope Benedict XVI has called for a hermeneutic of continuity in interpreting all Catholic teaching. There is no greater need for continuity than in the Sacred Liturgy. If we follow the official musical program given by the Church, we will immediately begin the process of restoring our Catholic Identity and revivifying the Sacred Treasury of our musical heritage. **Priests, however, must be at the forefront of this revival. If they do not sing their chants, then the solemn sung Liturgy can never be realized, no matter how magnificent the parish choir is.**

> ...We have a new Missal and the chants are now standardized in our Roman Tradition. **You do not have to be a professional musician.** You may not even know how to read music. You will have seven days to begin the process of understanding what you have to do...**Fathers, you not only are absolutely necessary to consecrate the Holy Eucharist**, you are also **absolutely necessary** for the **Mass to be sung properly** according to our Tradition!!!!![36]

Amen!

---

[36] http://www.chantcafe.com/2012/04/special-invitation-to-priests.html

The Sequence at Pentecost

Here's everything you ever wanted to know about the Sequence for Pentecost! This information comes to you from one who is much more knowledgeable than I am regarding such matters.

The question arises: is the Sequence for Pentecost sung *before* or *after* the Alleluia? This becomes an issue only for the *Novus Ordo*; the answer is quite clear in the Extraordinary Form.

Sigh. Welcome to the world of ecclesiastical politics.

The present state of affairs leaves us in the conundrum of both "A" and "B" (which are mutually exclusive) being correct (for now, at least), depending on *where* the Mass is being offered. Nevertheless it is important to know which of the two "correct" positions is the more appropriate.

The current (2011) English translation of the *General Instruction to the Roman Miss*al (*GIRM*), "Including Adaptations for Dioceses of the United States of America" states:

> 64. The Sequence, which is optional except on Easter Sunday and on Pentecost Day, is sung before the *Alleluia*.

The *GIRM* is liturgical law for the Roman Rite throughout the world. But note that this quotation (no. 64) is from the approved English translation of the *GIRM* that includes "Adaptations for Dioceses of the United States of America". When we compare this same article to the Latin original of the *GIRM* that is used throughout the rest of the world, we find exactly the opposite:

> 64. Sequentia, quae praeter quam diebus Paschae et Pentecostes, est ad libitum, cantatur post Allelúia.

(64. The Sequence, which is optional except on the days of Pascha and Pentecost, is sung after the *Alleluia*.)

Either the Vatican's designated approvers of official vernacular translations didn't catch the error in the English edition, or the change was approved as an authorized adaptation for Dioceses of the USA. I'm inclined to think that it was a case of the latter: the prelates appointed to oversee linguistics didn't have a background in sacred liturgy, let alone in sacred music. They failed to understand and appreciate what a *Sequentia* is, what it is meant to do, and why it is called "*Sequentia*": it follows *sequentially* after the Alleluia, as a florid jubilation on that same Alleluia.

Well-meaning priests and bishops had long noted (well, "long", anyway, after Pope Paul VI's new Mass came out in the 1970's) that, with the new – and misunderstood – emphasis on *everyone* having to sing the "Gospel Acclamation" (i.e., "Alleluia"), the people were all standing to sing the Alleluia, and then everyone had to "just" stand there while someone (often just a cantor, since the choir wouldn't learn to sing the Sequence) sang this long solo.

Or, worse yet (following down that rabbit trail of "active participation"), this is all viewed as the apparent anticlimax of the entire congregation having to stand (oh, my Gawd!) and recite (because we HAVE to "participate"!! – and because the chant is TOO HARD for the congregation to learn – and besides, chant is SO pre-Vatican Two!). Meanwhile the deacon/priest stands at the ambo "wasting his time", waiting for this unnecessary intrusion into HIS ministry of proclaiming the Gospel.

With this kind of mindset, coupled with sheer ignorance, the historical placement of the Sequence *after* the "Gospel Acclamation" made no sense whatsoever.

Ergo, *voilà*! We'll just move the Sequence to *before* the "Gospel Acclamation"...a sort of extended meditation, before we get on to the real business of the congregation leaping to its feet to "welcome" the Gospel. And this is what happens when you let "liturgists" (cf. "terrorists") run things.

So when it comes to the Sequence in the *Novus Ordo* Missae (i.e., ordinary form), the present state of affairs is dismal: in the USA, it is sung *before* the "Gospel Acclamation"; everywhere else in the Catholic world, it is sung in its rightful and historical place: *after* the Alleluia.

Churches Are Not Concert Halls

I know of two concerts held in churches in the last week or so (in different dioceses and different states); between the two of them, they violated these regulations: 1) the music was not exclusively sacred music; 2) the musicians were seated in the sanctuary; 3) in one case, the Blessed Sacrament was not removed; and 3) in one case, admission was charged for the concert.

These points are explicitly addressed in the document *Concerts in Churches* published by the Congregation for Divine Worship and the Sacraments in 1987 (see Appendix B). Let me address the violations using the words of the document (my **emphases**).

First, the music for both concerts was, from all reports, beautiful and beautifully performed. One concert included sacred music; the other was purely "contemporary Christian". However, the document notes that

> The most beautiful symphonic music, for example, **is not in itself** of religious character. **The definition of sacred or religious music depends explicitly on the original intended use of the musical pieces or songs,** and likewise on their content…(paragraph III.8.)

Second, the document also states unequivocally that, "**The musicians and the singers should not be placed in the sanctuary**" (paragraph III.10.e.).

Third, the document states, "The Blessed Sacrament should be, as far as possible, **reserved in a side chapel** or in another safe and suitably adorned place" (paragraph III.10.f.).

Finally, with regard to charging admission, the document says, "**Entrance to the church must be without payment and open to all**." (paragraph III.10.c.).

I've brought up the question of non-sacred music concerts in churches before...and I think perhaps I am beating my head against the proverbial brick wall.

Several people – including a bishop or two – have commented dismissively that they aren't concerned about this kind of abuse because, "they even do it in Rome". All righty, then. Following that kind of reasoning, we might say that, even though artificial contraception is against Church teaching, the vast majority of Catholics couples use it, probably "even in Rome". Does that make it okay?

Hmm. What's that quote from Venerable Archbishop Sheen? "Right is right, even if no one is right. Wrong is wrong, even if everyone is wrong."

Here are another couple of questions worth looking into: *Why* did the CDW issue that document, and *why* is it ignored?

The document answers the first question itself. In a paragraph sub-titled "The Character and Purpose of Churches", it says:

> According to tradition as expressed in the **rite for the dedication** of a church and altar, **churches are primarily places where the people of God gather**, and are "made one as the Father, the Son and the Holy Spirit are one, and are the Church, the temple of God built with living stones, **in which the Father is worshipped in spirit and in truth**." Rightly so, from ancient times the name "church" has been extended to the building in which the Christian community unite to hear the word of God, to pray together, to receive the sacraments, to celebrate the Eucharist and to prolong its celebration in the adoration of the Blessed Sacrament... (par. 5)

The church is a place where liturgical worship takes place. That is its primary purpose. The document continues:

> Churches, however, **cannot be considered simply as public places for any kind of meeting**. They are sacred places, that is, "**set apart**" in a permanent way for **divine worship** by their dedication and blessing.

In other words, a church is not a concert hall.

> As visible constructions, churches are signs of the pilgrim Church on earth; they are images that proclaim the heavenly Jerusalem, places in which are actualized the mystery of the communion between man and God. Both in urban areas and in the countryside, **the church remains the house of God**, and the sign of his dwelling among men. It remains a **sacred place**, **even when no liturgical celebration** is taking place.

Care must be taken to preserve that sacred place. That's why the document stipulates that "the performers and the audience must be dressed in a manner which is fitting to the sacred character of the place"; that "the musicians and the singers should not be placed in the sanctuary"; that "the greatest respect is to be shown to the altar, the president's chair and the ambo; and that "the Blessed Sacrament should be, as far as possible, reserved in a side chapel or in another safe and suitably adorned place".

In the "contemporary Christian music" concert mentioned above, the Blessed Sacrament remained in the tabernacle because the singer desired to be near Jesus. The article I read said that she pleaded for the Blessed Sacrament to remain, and she assured those responsible that there would be nothing in the concert that would offend Him.

I felt sad reading this. Some of the people involved are good friends of mine, and I have no doubts about their desire to live the faith fully, to be true to the teachings of the Church, and to bring others closer to God. And I suspect this singer was sincere in her love for Jesus and the Eucharist. I'm sure that all concerned sincerely believed that Jesus would be honored by the music. *They just didn't know any better.*

I'm convinced that Our Lord was pleased with that singer's devotion, and with the "good intentions" of the organizers. I don't think anyone there intended to disobey Church teaching or purposely offend God! On the other hand, I cannot believe that Jesus was pleased about the lack of understanding of why a concert of that nature should not be taking place in a church in the first place, especially with the musicians placed in the sanctuary.

Now, *why* do we see an ignorance of the "rules", and why, even when the rules are brought to the attention of those who need to know them, they continue to be flaunted? The CDW document suggests that maintaining the sense of sacredness of the church

> …will only be possible **in so far as churches maintain their specific identity.** When churches are **used for ends other than those** for which they were built, their role as a **sign of the Christian mystery is put at risk**, with more or less serious harm to the teaching of the faith and to the sensitivity of the People of God, according to the Lord's words: "My house is a house of prayer" (Lk 19:46).

I submit that the very architecture, furnishings, and treatment of our "modern" churches (meaning those built or remodeled post-Vatican II) does not lend itself to our understanding the nature and use of the sacred space. The priest stands behind the altar, facing the people; oftentimes the choir is situated in or next to the sanctuary; the tabernacle is often located such that you have to search for it; laymen in street clothes traipse through the sanctuary during Mass as extraordinary ministers of Holy Communion; the altar rails are gone.

In short, the boundaries of the sanctuary are blurred – both physically and spiritually.

The whole arrangement of the sanctuary in the current, common usage suggests a stage, but we could change all that pretty easily. If the faithful were more used to *ad orientem* worship, the focus would be changed, and the sanctuary could be seen as it is meant to be seen: as a space for the altar of God, where we offer our worship to Him, led by a priest who really acts like a *priest*, rather than a talk-show host. If the altar were treated more in keeping with its nature as well – as an altar of sacrifice; as an altar where the Real Presence of Jesus is brought at each Mass by the actions and prayers of the priest; an altar which retains its sacred nature *even when Mass is not being said* – then the idea of seating musicians around it, even if the Blessed Sacrament is removed from the tabernacle, would seem irreverent and disrespectful.

If we returned to *ad orientem* worship, vested the altar appropriately (instead of using it as a backdrop for floral arrangements), and had an altar rail marking off the boundary of the sanctuary, then using it as a stage would be unthinkable for most people. Explanations and rules would not be required. The faithful would *know* because they would have a heightened awareness of the sacredness of the sanctuary and altar.

And who knows? Perhaps we are headed in that direction! A 2012 article from the Catholic News Agency reported (my **emphases**):

> With the Vatican's approval on November 14 of its restructuring, the Congregation of Divine Worship and the Discipline of the Sacraments will shift its focus more intensely on art and liturgical music.
>
> The restructuring is in accord with a Sept. 2011 apostolic letter issued by Pope Benedict XVI, where he noted that the

changes will help the congregation in "giving a fresh impetus to **promoting the sacred liturgy** in the Church."

This will be achieved mainly through a new office dedicated to sacred music and liturgical art – **including architecture** – which will become operational next year.

Its charges will include issuing guidelines on liturgical music and the structure of new churches so that they **reflect the mysterious encounter with the divine**, as well as follow the dictates and instructions of the new English translation of the Roman Missal.

In his letter, the Pope wrote that these all must be in accord with the Second Vatican Council's "Constitution on the Sacred Liturgy." Overlooking that 1963 document has allowed for the **post-conciliar trend of building unedifying churches and filling them pop-influenced music.**[37]

Well, it's a start!

---

[37] http://www.catholicnewsagency.com/news/vatican-congregation-to-emphasize-liturgical-music-art/

Children's Mass and Music

When it comes to liturgical issues involving children, a priest I know has a ready comment: "'Cute' " trumps all," he tells me. I know he's right, but it doesn't stop me from making myself unpopular with lots of folks who think that there's nothing wrong with "cute" and that we should have more of it in the Mass.

I'm not talking here about the dismissal of children at Sunday Mass for a "children's liturgy of the word" to take place in another room (which is another issue). I'm talking primarily about the infamous "Children's Mass" and the infamous "children's" choir…and this is *not* to say that there is *not* a place for either. Both *can* be done properly, apparently (eyes rolling…sorry!). There does exist a *Directory for Masses with Children*[38], but, as seems to be the American way, it is much abused and disregarded.

The *Directory* describes acceptable norms and procedures for "Masses with Adults in which Children Participate" (which would be your typical Sunday Mass in most parishes), and "Masses with Children in which Only a Few Adults Participate" (which would be more along the lines of a daily Mass at a Catholic elementary school). I think the problem comes when the decision is made to have a Sunday Mass that looks like it falls into the second category, even though adults outnumber the children, and it's the main Sunday Mass of the parish. Granted, it may be absolutely true that few adults are *actually* participating, but given the fact that the *Directory* was prepared under the guidance of Monsignor Annibale Bugnini, it is unlikely that the chapter title refers to anything more than the number of warm adult bodies physically present in the church.

---

[38] See http://www.adoremus.org/DMC-73.html

So, here's the problem, made specific to the parish nearest to my home (which is not to say that it is the parish of which I consider myself a member, nor does it say I am even welcome there…which I am not…either one): On the first Sunday of every month from October to May, there is a "Children's Mass" – explicitly so called by the pastor of the parish. At this parish, there is only one Mass in English on Sundays, and this "Children's Mass" supplants the main, English Mass of the Sunday. I admit that I have not attended this Mass in a long, long time, but I know what it used to be like, and I've heard reports from reliable sources about recent occurrences. All reports indicate that things have gone from bad to worse. I notice that in the online parish bulletin, the pastor has decided this year to call it a "Youth Mass".

[Pause here for a moment of hair-pulling, teeth-gnashing, guttural noise-making, and even some outright shouting of "what is he THINKING!"…okay, I'm under control now. Let us continue.]

This first-Sunday-of-the-month Mass consists of music sung by a small children's choir. (Small children? Or a small choir? Ummm…both, actually…) What's wrong with that? After all, we have all seen some really good children's choirs on you-tube – kids singing Gregorian chant or even sacred polyphony. No, there's nothing wrong with that.

Unfortunately, the kids in our local "children's choir" are directed in singing little ditties along the lines of "Jesus Loves Me", and other songs that would qualify mostly as Protestant children's Bible songs, with little to recommend them to Catholic sensibilities. "But it's so *cute*!"

In my main attempt to change the pastor's mind about all this a few years ago, I wrote a letter to him, addressing the problems. In part, I said:

> …Generally speaking, the music chosen for the children to sing is not suitable to Mass; there seems to be an increasingly childish flavor to the songs, and some are of questionable theological soundness. Even young children can be taught to sing hymns that are more reverent and mature than those currently in use. After one of the last times my daughter sang in the children's choir, she spontaneously noted, "I don't think *Lord of the Dance* was really an appropriate song for communion." When I asked her for her reasons, she said that it was not slow and serious enough. A good appraisal, I think, "out of the mouths of babes." *Lord of the Dance* certainly is not conducive to pondering the mystery of the Eucharist.
>
> There also seems to be an increase in the use of hand gestures and body movements in the songs. While this can be amusing and entertaining in a children's performance, it is liturgically inappropriate. Bishop Vasa's pastoral letter, *Servant of the Sacred Liturgy,* p. 26, reads "No dancing (i.e., ballet, children's gestures as dancing…) is permitted to be 'introduced into liturgical celebrations of any kind whatever.' (*Notitiae II (1975) 202-205).*" The children themselves seem to be embarrassed at being asked to perform the gestures, and my daughter cites this as one reason she does not want to participate.
>
> Having the children sing at Mass takes on the appearance of a performance, rather than a ministry. In fact, a number of times, when you have thanked the children's choir for singing, the congregation breaks into applause for them. I

think this shows that the children's choir is not truly fulfilling a *ministry* in the minds of the adult members of the parish, and it is giving the children the wrong idea about what participation in the music ministry means. It is *not* about "performing" for the parents.

Lest you think I am totally "anti-children" (as the pastor has ~~accused~~ suggested) or that I am mean and stingy and unwilling to give credit where credit is due, here is the next-to-last paragraph of that same letter:

> I admire your desire to cultivate children's interest in music and singing; and I appreciate very much the fact that, as always, you are willing to go the "extra mile" to implement a good idea. Still, there are other, more appropriate, times for the children to display their talents. For instance, the children could be invited to perform during the Knights of Columbus breakfast after Mass on the second Sunday of each month; this would probably also have the effect of increasing attendance at that event. Alternatively, a special performance could be arranged on a weekday evening – perhaps even during the Wednesday night RE activities. Most people – myself included! – do like to hear young children sing, and I'm sure performances outside of Mass would be well-attended.

At the time I wrote that letter, the children's choir sang at the Sunday Mass, and that was that. It wasn't called a "Children's Mass"; it was just that we had the children singing. But now there is a change in the description in the bulletin: it is called the "Children's Mass" or the "Youth Mass", and we are told that the children will be found helping with every "ministry" available – and some "ministries" they are performing are simply not appropriate. In addition, there have been several times when, in lieu of a homily, Father had the children act out a skit which he narrated. I am also reminded of the time Father had all the children in attendance at Mass come up around the altar for the consecration!

[Pause again for more gnashing of teeth and rending of garments. Deep cleansing breaths…]

Tailoring a main Sunday Mass to the children is, in my ~~humble~~ opinion, reprehensible. It dumbs down the Mass, and this does not benefit the children any more than it benefits the adults. Even the *Directory* notes:

> 21. It is always necessary to keep in mind that these Eucharistic Celebrations must **lead children toward the celebration of Mass with adults, especially in the Masses at which the Christian community must come together on Sundays**… (my emphasis)

In other words, these "Masses with Children" should *not* be the Sunday Mass of the parish, and they should always lead children toward a more mature understanding of the liturgy. A "Children's Mass" on Sunday, where the children sing kids' Bible songs, "help" in preparing the altar, act out a skit for the homily, etc., does not fit the bill. It meets the requirements for neither the "Masses with Children in Which Only a Few Adults Participate", nor the "Masses with Adults in Which Children Participate". It is an anomaly.

Unfortunately, it is my suspicion that this anomaly takes place at many parishes around Christmas time…particularly that Christmas Eve Mass that many mistake for the annual community Christmas party.

Sigh.

Glimmers of Hope, Part 3

The Annual Sacred Music Colloquium

One giant glimmer of hope, especially for liturgical music, is the annual Sacred Music Colloquium sponsored by the Church Music Association of America (CMAA). At the CMAA website, the following description is given:

> The primary focus of the Colloquium is instruction and experience in chant and the Catholic sacred music tradition, participation in chant choirs, daily and nightly lectures and performances and daily celebrations of liturgies in both English and Latin. You are there not merely as an attendee but as an integral part of the greatest music you will ever experience. It will touch your heart and thrill your artistic imagination.
>
> Attendance is open to anyone interested in improving the quality of music in Catholic worship. Professional musicians will appreciate the rigor, while enthusiastic volunteer singers and beginners new to the chant tradition will enjoy the opportunity to study under an expert faculty. Those who choose not to sing at all but merely want to learn will find a once-in-a-lifetime opportunity to absorb the full ethos of a world of the best liturgical music.[39]

This Colloquium increases in popularity each year, and that means hundreds of people are learning about our rich heritage of liturgical music – especially Gregorian chant. Although I have not attended myself, Stephanie Swee, President of our local *Society of St. Gregory the Great*[40], shared her experience of a Sacred Colloquium XXII in 2012. She wrote:

---

[39] http://musicasacra.com/colloquium/
[40]The Society of Saint Gregory the Great is a membership association of Catholic

"For me it was a week I cannot match to any in memory. It seemed to be that for most participants, although, of course, I didn't meet every one of the more than 200 people there.

"General observations are: People from all over the country and, indeed, all over the world, came together in a bonding I have never experienced before. They sang – in the form of more than a half dozen choirs – chant and sacred polyphony for six different Masses, four in the Ordinary Form and two in the Extraordinary Form. They did this by practicing what would be sung that day and came up with amazing results.

"We had, of course, some excellent teachers and directors...There were three chant levels: beginners; those who needed some refresher work; and the scholas. This made six groups divided by male and female voices. Between them, they did all the chant propers for the Masses, while polyphony groups did some "part" propers. Some days the ordinaries were sung in chant, some days in polyphony. For the chant ordinaries, no one even practiced (except perhaps for the beginners); it was assumed we all knew them well enough to sing them 'cold'. And it turned out fine.

"In addition to singing practice and instruction, there were lectures and presentations on church music documents, conducting, and numerous other topics. If one had wished, one could have been busy from the 8:15 morning prayer until 10pm, when some concerts and films concluded. Mass was at 5:15pm on the weekdays, and at 11am on Saturday and Sunday...

"Due to hard work and a lot of talent, the Masses were glorious. The chaplain for CMAA, Father Paisley, was very well trained in singing and the EF form. He is pastor of a parish in New Jersey, which is the

---

laity in the Diocese of Baker, Oregon, formed in 2008 to promote divine worship in accordance with the Supreme Magisterium of the Church.

only diocesan parish in the country dedicated to the older form of Mass.

"Our director was Jeffrey Morse, who is choirmaster for St. Stephen's Church in Sacramento, CA. He has a choir of 25-30 and a small group of young choristers. He was very disciplined in his approach, but very amusing also. Without getting too technical, Jeffrey initiated us into some 9th-century chant interpretations to use with the notation that Solesmes reformed in the last century. Often, just rehearsing took a lot of time, as we had some difficult things to do. However, the other members of the group I was with were very skilled, and after one day, it was hard to tell none of us had ever sung together before.

"Lunches outside allowed some of us to come back together and talk. Universally there was a sense of happiness and peace I have never seen in such a large group. We also had two dinners at which we eagerly shared thoughts with other attendees. I met at least five people with whom I intend to continue a relationship, including a woman from Michigan with nine children, who is carrying her parish musically. There were others, especially two priests with whom I had some good discussions.

"The Mass on Wednesday was a solemn high requiem in the extraordinary form, said for all deceased members of the CMAA, including Msgr. Schuler, who started all this. It was incredibly beautiful, especially the sequence, *Dies Irae*, sung alternately by men and woman. Although our schola has practiced that Mass, I hadn't sung it at an actual liturgy in more than 50 years. The parishioners who attended seemed stunned by the beauty of the music.

"The Cathedral is also beautiful, but has had some regrettable renovations, such as removal of the side altars. This meant that the priests there had no place to say their own Masses, but some did concelebrate at the *Novus Ordo* liturgies. Since that is not done in EF Masses, though, they had to say Mass in their hotel rooms for the most part.

"The Cathedral also has a large set of choir stalls, normally used as overflow seating, but which was perfect for our purposes. The men's schola could face the women's schola and alternate the way it should be done. The frescoes on walls are wonderful and the stained glass windows and marble breathtaking. The acoustics are very good, also. We never got a visit from the bishop, but I guess he was occupied elsewhere.

"In addition to the music practicums, we had lectures we could take in each morning and afternoon and also an hour talk from some of the presenters before Mass each weekday. Also, I should mention the Madeleine Choir School. It is a day school for young people who have talent and the desire to sing good sacred music. The director is fabulous. The choir performed in concert on Tuesday night with fourteen selections of the most glorious polyphony and hymns I have ever heard in one place. Only Salt Lake City and Boston have such a school, although the Lyceum Catholic School in Ohio has a wonderful schola of young people as well."

The Sacred Music Colloquium: The Masses, Part 1

This description is also courtesy of Stephanie Swee; here, she focuses on the Masses that took place during the Colloquium:

"During the six days of the event, there were six Masses and one solemn Vespers. There was morning and evening prayer most days as well, but those occasions featured simple psalmody sung alternately by men and women and did not require much work on anyone's part, since most of those who attended knew how to sing the Office.

"Of the Masses celebrated, four were in the ordinary form and two in the extraordinary. All had music in Latin, except for a couple of English motets and one English hymn. Some of the celebrants used Latin responses, some English. The last ordinary form Mass sung was on Sunday, July 1, and was the regular 11am Cathedral parish Mass for the 13th Sunday in Ordinary Time. It was also the longest of all the Masses.

"The polyphonic choir sang a Monteverdi ordinary. This is a work in five parts and is unearthly in its beauty. The propers were the regular chant ones for the day and the *Introit* for that Sunday was from Psalm 46, "*Omnes gentes, plaudite minibus*" (All you nations, clap your hands"). As with all the other Masses, the *Introit* was started as the procession entered, the way it is supposed to be sung, and the choir continued it while the ministers assembled and the celebrant incensed the altar. As with most of the Masses, Father Paisley, the chaplain of CMAA, sang the Mass. He is a pastor from New Jersey whose diocesan parish celebrates Mass always in the extraordinary form – the only such parish in the country.

"The men's group sang the *Gradual* - "Venite, filii, audite me" ("Come, children, hearken unto me") and the *Alleluia* following it. In the ordinary form, the *Gradual* follows the first reading and *Alleluia* the second, where many churches use first the Responsorial psalm and then the common Alleluia.

"Those in the congregation who knew it were invited to join in Credo III, probably the easiest and most familiar of the sung Latin professions of faith. After the Offertory, "*Sicut in holocaust*" ("As a holocaust of rams and bullocks ... let our sacrifice be in your sight this day"), the polyphonic choir sang a motet by Morales, *O Sacrum Convivium*. The *Sanctus* by Monteverdi followed the Preface and the *Agnus Dei* came just before Communion. It was interesting to see how the Latin propers, written for the older form of the Mass, could fit just as easily into the *Novus Ordo.*

"The *Communion,* as in all six Masses, was sung with both antiphon and verses of the psalm. When the choir finished a certain number of verses, the magnificent organ of the Cathedral took over and played variations on the melody until all had received the Eucharist. Then a motet was usually sung; on Sunday it was the Bruckner *Ave Maria.*

"As far as one could tell, the congregation seemed to be happy with the celebration. Although those in the colloquium were all urged to consider receiving Communion kneeling and on the tongue, there were priests distributing the sacrament for those who wished to receive standing and in the hand. In the Extraordinary Form Masses, of course, one must receive the host on the tongue."

The Colloquium Masses, part 2

Stephanie Swee continues her observations, this time on the extraordinary form Masses that were said at the Sacred Music Colloquiuum in 2012.

"For some of those attending the Sacred Music Colloquium in Salt Lake City, the two extraordinary form Masses were the highlights of the week. On Wednesday, a Requiem Mass was celebrated for the deceased members of the organization. The *Requiem Missa Cantata* was splendidly sung by a number of choirs, and the well-known sequence, *Dies Irae*, was magnificent in its rendition by alternating chant choirs of men and women. Even though the celebrant wore black, the mood was joyous, as the comforting chants of the Mass for the Dead, such as the haunting Introit, *Requiem aeternam*, moved all those in attendance.

"Some young friends who drove an hour to be at the Requiem Mass were speechless after the last strains of music died away. They had never, they said, heard anything so beautiful – until the Friday extraordinary Mass, which they said exceeded even what they had experienced on Wednesday.

"The Friday, June 29, liturgy was a Solemn High Mass in honor of Saints Peter and Paul. The vestments were red velvet and the music included a polyphonic ordinary by Louis Vierne, his *Missa Solennelle, Opus 16*. Although those parts were very elaborate, just as impressive were the proper chants, especially the Communion, *Tu es Petrus,* with its psalm verses.

"A motet by Sir John Hawkins followed the distribution of communion, *Quem dicunt hominess* ("Who do men say is the Son of man; You are Christ, the Son of the living God"). After Mass (since English cannot be sung during the span of the liturgy in the extraordinary form) a motet in the vernacular, which echoed the previous one, served as recessional: *The Son of Man*, composed by Sir Richard Newman.

"There was a noticeable hush after this Mass, when it seemed those in attendance were still stunned by the solemnity of the rite and the music. One young man who had grown up in Salt Lake City and become a convert from Mormonism to Catholicism there, said he felt as if he were dreaming: "I never thought I would see a Mass like this in the Cathedral," he said.

"There was in all the Masses a liberal use of incense and candles. Just as the organ sometimes became overwhelming in its volume, the ministers pulled out all the stops in the use of ceremonials.

"It is true that many of the colloquium attendees came from rich musical backgrounds, some directors of choirs, many with advanced degrees in music. But others were neophytes and some had never sung chant before. It was a testament to the power of the liturgy and of its proper music that all could come together in this solemn act of worship, to praise God and offer again the sacrifice of Calvary."

Section V:

The Extraordinary Form of the Mass

It has a beauty to it that is beyond discussion, at least to reasonable people. It conveys in a strong way that it is Christ Himself who is making the sacrifice for us on Calvary. There's a strong sense in the Extraordinary Form of the Mass of the transcendent, in other words, that Heaven is meeting earth in these treasured of the offering of the Eucharistic sacrifice.

There's no question that there remains in certain places a resistance to do what the Holy Father has asked, and that's sad.
It's sometimes even an expression of disagreement with the Holy Father's discipline, and even the expression that this is harmful to the Church.

Raymond Cardinal Burke
in a Catholic News Agency video

Why I Promote the EF Mass

I am a tireless promoter of the Extraordinary Form of the Mass.

In fact, I really think "promoting" the EF Mass is not enough. I think instruction and participation in the EF Mass really should be *required* of all Catholics. Yes, I know, that's pretty extreme. I'll try to explain.

I barely know how to express what I feel when I attend an EF Mass. I find it hauntingly beautiful, spiritually uplifting, other-worldly…a host of other adjectives. Perhaps the word I'm searching for is – wait for it! – "ineffable"? Let's see: "Ineffable: Too great or extreme to be expressed or described in words; too sacred to be uttered". Yes, that pretty well sums it up. No wonder Bishop Donald Trautman doesn't want us to use that word.[41]

But these "feelings" I get at the EF Mass are not the reason why I think the EF Mass needs to be promoted, explained, and offered to the Catholics who've never experienced it. Oh yes, I do want others to feel what I feel, but it is certainly possible that some will *never* get that sense of ineffability. Still, they need to have the experience. They need to understand more about the EF Mass.

Why? Because we do not remain children all our lives. And because it is essential to our Catholic identity.

> About this we have much to say, and it is difficult to explain, for you have become sluggish in hearing. Although you should be teachers by this time, you need to have someone teach you again the basic elements of the utterances of God.

---

[41] For those unaware, Bishop Trautman waged quite a war against the New Translation, and one word that came up often was "ineffable", which he maintained was not a word the lay faithful found familiar or easily defined. See one of Fr. Z's commentaries at http://wdtprs.com/blog/2009/11/bp-donald-ineffable-trautmans-jihad-against-the-new-translation/

> You need milk, (and) not solid food. Everyone who lives on milk lacks experience of the word of righteousness, for he is a child. But solid food is for the mature, for those whose faculties are trained by practice to discern good and evil. (Hebrews 5:11-14)

Many years ago, I worked at a daycare center. One little girl had been in a serious car accident at age three years; she'd been badly burned and almost died, and recuperated at home for months. Then came the big day when she returned to daycare, scars and all. And she arrived with a problem her mom wanted us to help correct: she would consume only milk. She did not want to eat any solid food. This was the result of her trauma, the pain she experienced, the fact that she could not tolerate solid food for a while, etc. Now she was 4 years old, thin as a rail, and she needed to eat "real" food. Slowly we were able to wean her away from her milk and get her to eat the same foods the other children were offered for lunch and snack.

But this little girl was resistant to our efforts…*very* resistant. She wanted her milk. Similarly, many adults in our Church are resistant to the "solid food" of "real" worship. They want their bottle of milk, the "comfortable" Mass they've become accustomed to, with the 4-hymn sandwich, the fluffy homily, and the feel-good atmosphere. They don't want to be challenged, they don't want to have to chew on the meat of some spiritual truth, and they don't want to have to think about what the Mass really means. They "know all that" – but not really.

I know there are devout people who attend the *Novus Ordo* Mass and have a healthy spiritual life. Despite liturgical abuses and impoverished homilies, they experience some sense of the ineffable in the NO Mass. And these people have expressed this thought to me, wondering why I still push the EF Mass; they assure me that they are indeed being challenged and are growing spiritually. I believe them.

Still…the Mass is where earth touches Heaven; Mass should give us a glimpse of Heaven, at least in some small sense. I want that glimpse to be as clear and sharp as possible, and I think the EF Mass accomplishes that task better than the *Novus Ordo*.

Consider this analogy: Think of best vacation spot you've ever visited (or the most sublime sunset you've experienced, or the most exquisite meal you've ever eaten; any indescribable experience will do, but let's stick with the vacation analogy). Now imagine describing this vacation spot and your experience of it to someone who has never been there. Your words will not substitute for their own personal experience. They may say, "Oh yes, I went to a place like that one time", or "Yes, I can imagine how beautiful that would be." But their imagination will fall short of the actual experience. If you have photos, that will help – it will bring their experience close to yours. And video footage will bring them even closer. But still, they will not have *experienced* the physical reality of that vacation spot.

It's kind of the same thing with Heaven. We can't experience Heaven here on earth.

> [A]s it is written: "What eye has not seen, and ear has not heard, and what has not entered the human heart, what God has prepared for those who love him," this God has revealed to us through the Spirit (1 Corinthians 2:9, citing Isaiah 64:3)

The Mass is supposed to help us imagine what God has prepared for us.

Here's a description of the beatific vision – the direct knowledge of God which the angels and the souls of the just enjoy in Heaven:

Imagine a man in whom the tumult of the flesh goes silent, in whom the images of earth, of water, of air and of the skies cease to resound. His soul turns quiet and, self-reflecting no longer, it transcends itself. Dreams and visions end. So too does all speech and every gesture, everything in fact which comes to be only to pass away. All these things cry out: "We did not make ourselves. It is the Eternal One who made us." And after they have said this, think of them falling silent, turning to listen to the One Who created them. And imagine Him speaking. Speaking Himself, so that we could hear His word, not in the language of the flesh, not through the speech of an angel, not by way of a rattling cloud or a mysterious parable. But Himself. The One Whom we love in everything. Imagine we could hear Him without them. Reaching out with speeding thought we come to Him, to the Eternal Wisdom which outlasts everything. And imagine if sight of Him were kept available, while all lesser sights were taken away. Think of this encounter, seizing, absorbing, drawing the witness into the depths of joy. Eternal life would be of a kind with this moment of understanding. (from Book IX of St. Augustine's *Confessions*)

Now, *that's* Heaven. It's not the Disneyland Heaven we describe to little children, who can only tolerate "milk". It is the Heaven of the justified, purified soul, which yearns for and finally obtains the beatific vision.

The EF Mass brings us closer to that Heavenly reality. It is structured to reach ever upward, whereas the NO has the tendency to be bogged down in human affairs and focus on our own earthly existence. (Yes, I know, the NO can be said reverently and experienced at a higher level than most people do, but it is also much more susceptible to liturgical abuse and a focus on the human rather than the divine.)

I want the EF Mass available to everyone, not just to me. I want it introduced, explained, promoted, and provided for all the faithful. I want this because the Eucharist is the source and summit of our Christian lives, because the Mass is our highest form of worship, and because the Sacred Liturgy is who we are as Catholics.

Our "source and summit" doesn't flow from simple ditties sung to folk guitar accompaniment; our highest form of worship is not dignified by liturgical dance, hand-clapping-foot-tapping music, or impromptu prayers adlibbed by Father Feelgood; and our Catholic identity is not captured by imitating Protestant worship that lacks the fundamental understanding of the Real Presence of Jesus in the Eucharist, or the true understanding of the Church as the Bride of Christ.

I want the EF Mass because by saving the liturgy, we *will* save the world.

How about you? Are you ready for some" solid food"?

Seven Reasons Why You Should *Not* Go to the Traditional Latin Mass

I promote the Traditional Latin Mass as often as I have a chance. And yet, I know that there is great danger in store, especially for those who have known only the *Novus Ordo*. The TLM opens eyes and hearts to the beauty and mystery of our Catholic faith, and when that happens, there is bound to be some pain involved...especially when one is forced to return to the impoverished version of the *Novus Ordo* Mass that is celebrated in the vast majority of parishes (in my experience).

So to give you fair warning, here are seven reasons *not* to go to the Traditional Latin Mass.

1. **It will make you wonder why we have lay ministers of Holy Communion.**

If it's the same Mass, and it's the same Jesus in each Mass, then why is it that in the extraordinary form of the Mass (the TLM, as it is often called), *only the priest* may handle the Body and Blood of Our Lord? Could it be because (gasp) he is *ordained* for that purpose? Could it be that his hands are anointed for that purpose? Could it be because he is a...*priest?* Once you experience that a few times, it starts to look quite unsettling to see lay ministers – or even deacons and acolytes – distributing Holy Communion, or purifying the vessels (which they're not supposed to do anyway), or just in general traipsing through the sanctuary. Those things don't happen in the TLM, and it makes a huge difference in one's sense of reverence and awe during the Mass.

2. **It will make you more aware of the Real Presence of Jesus in the Eucharist.**

Precisely *because* the priest is the only one who may handle the Eucharist, awareness is instantly raised as to the importance of that little "wafer" – the True Body of Christ. Because the faithful receive on the tongue while kneeling, reverence is cultivated. It cannot be otherwise. Receiving Holy Communion becomes more humbling. It makes one more aware of Jesus and what He does for us by coming to us in the Eucharist. Truly.

3. It will make you wonder why we have guitar music at Mass.

After a period of adjustment, as your musical "palate" is cleansed of the sugary sweet pop tunes of OCP (Oregon Catholic Press) origin, Gregorian chant will impress its spiritual flavor on your heart and mind, and you will experience the way in which this sacred music – which was designed for *nothing but the worship of God* – lifts your soul to God.

4. It will bring you to a new understanding of the liturgical worship of the Catholic Church.

The interior logic and spiritual integrity of the extraordinary form will manifest itself to you over a period of time. It is an integrity that no longer exists in the *Novus Ordo* – at least as it is celebrated in most parishes. And even in the best of situations, you will sense, after some time, that there is something missing in the *Novus Ordo*. Part of that has to do with the abbreviated nature of the prayers; yes, the new translation is a good start, but the prayers are still…well…incomplete, when compared with those of the extraordinary form.

5. It will bring you to a new awareness of your own sinfulness…and it will make you more Catholic in your understanding of Church teaching on things like homosexuality, abortion, and artificial contraception.

The prayers of the extraordinary form talk about sin (and some of this sense of our sinfulness has been restored with the new translation). The sung Kyrie is an extended plea for mercy. The prayers at the foot of the altar and the *Confiteor* are much richer and piercing than anything in the Ordinary Form. Read the prayers of the TLM. How does this relate to an increase in understanding of Church teaching? I don't know, exactly. But it does.

6. **It will make you aware of how "horizontal" the worship is in the NO.**

I'm talking here about the typical experience of the NO in the typical parish in my experience. It's flat. It's not aimed upwards; we aim it at each other. The priest faces us; we interrupt our worship to extend the "sign of peace", which in some parishes is tantamount of a free-for-all of pious handshaking and smiling and crawling over each other to greet everyone. The songs chosen (instead of the music proper to the Mass) are sometimes of questionable theology, and often are pure "schmaltz", playing on our more secular emotions rather than lifting our minds and hearts to God. Why? Because they resemble secular music – not sacred music.

7. **It will make you hunger and thirst for true worship every time you attend the typical *Novus Ordo* Mass at your parish.**

This is because, as one blogger put it, "the two Masses are as different as chalk is to cheese"[42]. Even in a *Novus Ordo* that is said properly – even with the Gregorian chant propers and ordinary, even with the priest celebrating the Mass *ad orientem* – it is quite likely that you will feel that *something is missing.* Because it is.

So…In short, you should **not** attend the TLM because it will make you **more aware of your Catholic identity**. And that is precisely what the enemy does **not** want.

---

[42] Richard Collins at http://linenonthehedgerow.blogspot.com/

Even if you decide, after my dire warnings, that you'd like to try the TLM, the enemy still has a few tricks up his sleeve for you. You see, if you've had a long history of attending the *Novus Ordo*, and if you enjoy singing the songs from the *JourneySong Book* or *Breaking Bread* or any of the others of that ilk, you will *not* experience the effects listed here immediately. It would take some time before the changes could take hold. So if you go just one time, you might feel like a fish out of water; it may seem odd and quiet and just plain different. And since we are human, and humans don't like change, you will quite likely say, "I guess it's fine for all those trad types, but it's just not for me."

(And that's part of the problem, too. The *Novus Ordo* should *not* seem so very different from the TLM – not if we really had a "hermeneutic of continuity" happening here. But we don't.)

So, if you are forced to attend a TLM, or if you go *once* just to prove you gave it a shot, fear not. You may be quite able to hold onto your Protestantized view of worship, and you will be able to continue to speak disparagingly of the use of Latin and the fact that you can't understand the words (but if you know how to read, you have no excuse, because there will be, almost certainly, an English-Latin booklet available for you to refer to).

If you really give the TLM a try, though – because maybe you seek a greater "actual" participation in the Mass, and you are a Catholic who wants to truly be *Catholic* – you *will* experience all of the above effects, and they really are good things and not bad.

But a word of warning is still in order:

Once you experience the effects noted, you will probably talk about them. And then you will probably be criticized, if not ostracized, by many in your parish. You'll hear endless arguments about how you are being "divisive" and not promoting the unity of the Body of

Christ in your parish or diocese. And you will not be happy about this. It will hurt.

But I'll tell you something: it's worth every bit of the pain.

How to Undermine the TLM in Your Parish

The previous chapter ("Seven Reasons You Should NOT Go to the TLM") was aimed primarily at the lay faithful. The laity must be warned about this monster lurking in the closet!

This chapter is aimed at pastors. Pastors who are convinced that the TLM will lead to all sorts of unseen and unwanted side effects in their parishioners are advised to take the following steps to deter any efforts to get a TLM established, or to undermine one that is already celebrated with any sort of regularity.

N.B.: Some pastors *inadvertently* engage in some of these hindrances. I hope such good shepherds will see these notes as a warning as to what to avoid if they want the TLM to flourish in their parishes.

That said, here are my suggestions for undermining the TLM:

1. Arrange the schedule so that the time and date of the next TLM is almost impossible to ascertain more than one hour in advance. For instance, the TLM could be scheduled at any of these times:

   a. At 3:47 pm on alternate Sundays unless there is a youth Mass that week. In that case the TLM time and location will be announced at 3pm, at the beginning of the Youth Mass.

   b. At noon on the first and third Sundays of the month, unless there's a Spanish Mass at 11, in which case the TLM will be moved to 1 pm; or unless the priest has to celebrate Mass at one of the mission churches, in which case the TLM will be moved to 3pm; or unless there is a choir practice for the children's Mass, in which case the

TLM will be cancelled. Announce the particular circumstances of that week's TLM at the 9:30 am Mass, during the announcements.

   c. Every fifth Sunday when there is a full moon; no need to announce a time and location, because there will almost never be a fifth Sunday with a full moon.

2. Do not allow or encourage any Latin in the main Masses of the parish, and allow and encourage those parishioners who are willing to bad-mouth it and talk about how Latin is a step backwards in the progress of the Church.

3. If you are the pastor, and it is your associate who says the TLM, make sure he experiences last minute schedule changes that require, "sadly", that the TLM be cancelled that week. A motivated pastor can make sure this happens every week.

4. Require the TLM crowd to conspicuously attend the *Novus Ordo* Masses in your parish, in order to prove that they are giving the NO a chance, and are willing to be a part of the community. Do not require the NO crowd to attend any TLMs, though.

5. After a few months of the irregular scheduling described in #1, and the additional effects of #2-4, allow a TLM to actually take place. "Sadly" note the dwindling (or perhaps even non-existent) attendance, and announce that, given the lack of interest, the TLM will no longer be offered.

6. If you don't know how to say the TLM, use that as an excuse, and say that you do not have the time or ability to

learn Latin. Do not let any parishioners know the extreme measures you have taken to learn and offer the Mass in Spanish (or Vietnamese, or any other language), however. (Be sure to ignore or suppress those who mention that Canon Law requires seminaries to teach Latin.)

7. If all else fails, say that the bishop will not allow you to offer the TLM due to complaints received by those who don't want it in "their" parish.

There you have it: seven easy steps to squelching the TLM in your parish! These are bound to do the trick, and you might even just "lose" those pesky veil-wearing, communion-kneeling, tongue-receiving, traditional-minded trouble-makers to another parish in the process. Make sure you send this list on to the next pastor who has to deal with them.

Paving the Way for the EF Mass

Okay, enough messing around with trying to satirize the shenanigans that go on as *some* priests and bishops attempt to subvert the legitimate spiritual desires of the faithful to have free and ready access to the extraordinary form of the Mass.

What can we do that is constructive and positive?

I'm presenting here an outline of a program that I think could work in many parishes – provided, of course, that a willing pastor is available. There are two main goals. The first is to bring the parish to a more reverent celebration of the *Novus Ordo* through the re-introduction of chant, the use of the Latin ordinary, and the use of the Mass propers.

The second goal is to pave the way for the introduction and promotion of the EF Mass as a rite that is just as valid (if not more so…but we won't go there right now) as the NO. The EF Mass deserves to have a *prominent* place in the Mass schedule – rather than being relegated to a time slot that is unconventional and inconvenient for most. And I believe that if the pastor of a parish wants to lead his flock into an understanding of why this is so, he can do it. It may take some time and effort, but it can be done.

 In my parish, the pastor has shown great willingness to provide the EF Mass for us – putting in the time and effort to learn to celebrate it, and offering it every Sunday for almost a year, despite his very demanding schedule. For various reasons, though, we do not see our little group growing. I think it *could* grow, though, if the rest of the parishioners were appropriately catechized about the EF Mass, and if the liturgical celebrations of the parish as a whole were moved toward greater reverence and a stronger reflection of our Catholic identity.

This outline, created for the particular circumstances of my parish, can be adapted for any set of circumstances and Mass schedules. I haven't included anything about the Spanish Masses said in the parish, but it would be a good goal, I think, to also introduce the suggested changes into the Masses said in languages other than English (or Latin).

Also, my parish had a liberal pastor for over 15 years, and the people still suffer from their exposure to the happy-clappy liturgical abuses he allowed (encouraged?). A parish with less liberal baggage might move more quickly through the suggested changes; one with more baggage will pose more of a challenge. The pastor will have to exercise his own discernment as to how quickly changes can be made.

Here's the program:

1. **Start using a Latin chant ordinary at least once per month at Sunday Mass (i.e., Kyrie, Gloria, Sanctus, Agnus Dei), and introduce a sung Credo.**

   Why:
   a. To help the choir learn the Latin ordinary
   b. To accustom the people to the Latin ordinary
   c. To prepare the people for the extraordinary form of the Mass
   d. To accustom the people to singing the Credo

2. **Use the *Simple English Propers*[43] instead of the usual songs sung at Mass**

   Why:
   a. These are more in line with the new translation

---

[43] http://musicasacra.com/sep/

b. To foster a return to a more liturgically correct use of music in the Mass (that is, use of the proper chants designated by the Church as appropriate for each week's Sunday liturgy)

c. To foster our Catholic identity by preventing use of questionable hymns and musical styles

3. Gradually integrate the above into the way the Mass is celebrated currently:

Method:

a. Sing an "entrance hymn", but before the priest begins Mass, have the choir (or cantor) sing the introit from the *Simple English Propers*.

b. Instead of a hymn for Communion, use the proper of the day. Start with singing the Simple English Proper, with verses. At some point, add a Latin hymn. Progress to the Latin chant propers.

c. Introduce these changes first at the 7am Sunday Mass when a cantor is available; also introduce Latin propers at 7am Sunday Mass occasionally. [This suggestion is specific to my parish; this is a sparsely attended Mass and the people may be more amenable to the Latin propers.]

4. Slowly introduce *ad orientem* worship.

Purpose: To take the focus off of the priest as an individual, and to re-educate the people that Mass is totally focused on Our Lord, with all facing God as the priest offers our prayers.

Method: Begin at lower-attendance Masses, such as a Saturday evening Mass, or a 7am Sunday Mass; at each, introduce *ad orientem* at one Mass per month, then every two weeks, then every week. Progress to one Sunday/month at 9:30 (or main) Mass. Catechesis may be by way of bulletin inserts and explanation from pulpit. Also, a workshop could be held to explain it and deal with fall-out.

5. **Gradually, and without making a show of it, phase out female altar servers and recruit boys. Use cassock and surplice once all servers are male.**

Why: To promote vocations, which are sadly lacking in many dioceses! Also, the cassock and surplice are head-and-shoulders above the standard hooded alb (which makes the kids look like something out of "Snow White and the Seven Dwarves") in terms of fostering reverence and respect for the liturgy.

6. **Select, recruit, and train men and boys to serve at EF Mass.**

Why: to be celebrated well, the EF Mass needs servers. They must be male. Training the younger crowd in the EF Mass is another way to foster vocations, as well as fostering an increased reverence and appreciation for the Real Presence of Jesus in the Eucharist.

7. **Introduce bulletin "blurbs" about the EF Mass, explaining that it will become a regular part of the parish's worship, even beyond the EF Masses currently scheduled at the less desirable times (e.g., Sundays at 1pm).**

8. **After a suitable period of introducing these changes, announce that the EF Mass will be celebrated at 9:30am**

once per month; on those Sundays, the *Novus Ordo* Mass will be available at 1pm for those who prefer it. (Can you hear the shrieks even as we mention the very thought?!)

Really, I think this could work…but only if the priest is excited about it. He will have to be strong, because he will face unrest and discontent from parishioners, who will complain to the bishop. And if the bishop errs on the side of political correctness, the priest will be persecuted. Stand by him! Encourage him! Pray for him!

Pray for all the clergy.

Nothing Compares to the TLM

Note: I use the terms extraordinary form of the Mass, EF Mass, Traditional Latin Mass, and TLM interchangeably.

*** *** *** *** ***

My husband and I went to a *Novus Ordo* Mass last Saturday evening; with the extraordinary form not available to us, we were forced once again to choose the least offensive Mass we could find in our area. (See "Why I Dread Sunday Mass", p. 77)

The previous Sunday, we were able to attend Mass in the extraordinary form. Aaaahhh. It was good. But having to attend an NO Mass this past week brought the contrast all too sharply into focus.

I'm reading a book recommended to me by a friend: *The Desolate City: Revolution in the Catholic Church*, by Anne Roche Muggeridge (RIP), published originally in 1986. One review of the book suggests that the author's main thesis is "that an anti-Catholic revolution has taken place in the Church and that since 1968 various local and national sectors of the Church have fallen *de facto* into the hands of revolutionaries" [44].

Sadly, Muggeridge's commentary on the state of the Church is as true today (if not more so) than it was 25 years ago. And she speaks my mind exactly in some places. For instance, in mentioning that there *was* one priest who managed to say the NO Mass in a reverent and orthodox way, she still concludes that (my **emphases** throughout):

> Thankful as one is for a decent place to go to Mass, this situation is destructive not only because of its necessary

---

[44] http://www.rtforum.org/lt/lt27.html; see also the review at http://www.ad2000.com.au/articles/1988/apr1988p17_541.html

impermanence, but also because it has led to a revival of Donatism, whereby one finds oneself **sitting out Holy Communion if one has doubts about the validity of the Mass in progress**, and judging the validity of the Mass by the way the priest says it. This is dreadful. One is forced to fall back upon Catholic legislation worked out long ago to deal with situations like this, though it seems to lead in a circle. The Mass is **valid if said according to the mind of the Church**. But how does one know if the priest is actually saying it according to the Church's understanding? In general, the **outward sign of inward accord is adherence to the Church's rule of worship**. But **what if the priest departs** significantly from the prescribed form in the wide extra-legal fashion **tolerated by most bishops**? And far more serious, **what if the Church's legal form of worship is theologically divided against itself?** (p. 134-135)

One big difference between the NO Mass and the EF Mass is the ostensible change in the focus of the worship. In the EF Mass, the focus is God, pure and simple. Everything points upward, lifting our minds and souls from our earthly lives and encouraging us to look to our heavenly homeland. In the NO Mass…well…not so much – at least as I have seen it celebrated. We are focused more on *ourselves*, and everything is brought down to our level. The lines between the clergy and the laity are blurred as unvested lay faithful traipse through the sanctuary, serving as readers and extraordinary ministers of Holy Communion; we face the priest as an audience facing a talk-show host; we turn to each other (e.g., at the sign of peace), and hold each other's hands (at the Our Father); we listen as someone reads the bulletin just before the end of Mass (for fear that we will neglect to read its very important contents on our own); and we show up for Mass in attire that anticipates our afternoon recreation rather than the Heavenly banquet spread before us.

At an NO Mass as it is typically celebrated in my geographical area, I try to keep my head down and my eyes closed. I find it jarring to see a lay person handling the Eucharist as a minister of Holy Communion. I find it jarring even to see a deacon or acolyte doing so! And I find it jarring to see the deacon, acolyte, or lay ministers purifying the vessels after Communion. Isn't this the same Body of Christ we have in the Extraordinary Form of the Mass? Of course it is! So why is it permissible for Mary Quite Contrary (who refuses to use masculine nouns and pronouns in the *Credo*) to handle the Eucharist and the sacred vessels in the NO Mass, while *only the priest* does so in the EF Mass? At the NO Mass, I lower my head in embarrassment that we would subject the King of the Universe to such disrespect.

And there is so much noise! Almost everything in the NO Mass is said aloud, and yet, so much *is missing* in what is said. It may seem strange, but I miss the prayers that the priest prays in the EF Mass, *even though I never hear them spoken out loud*. In addition, having everything said in English detracts from the mystical reverence that I sense in the EF Mass. It brings it all down to our earthly level, rather than bringing us up to the heavenly banquet.

Muggeridge says she believes that the NO Mass "was devised by ideologues and installed by dupes" (p. 135), but that she still believes that the NO Mass is valid when celebrated according to the mind of the Church. Yet, there is a problem, and she perfectly captures the dilemma of the faithful Catholic who must tolerate a poorly-celebrated NO Mass:

> …I think that the paradigm shift attempted by the revolution is nowhere more clearly or **dangerously taught than in the reformed liturgy**, but I also believe, **as I must if I wish to remain Catholic**, that the Holy Ghost has not allowed His Church on earth to lose its power to make present perpetually

the Sacrifice of the Cross. **Therefore, I go to the new Mass**…although I know from experience that attendance **demands a constant struggle to maintain the Catholic world view against the current liturgical expression of it**. It is difficult to imagine a more ironic religious predicament. (p. 135)

She is not alone – not when she wrote those words, and not in the present! There are many people who have been struggling with the impoverished NO Mass for decades. Me? I have only struggled with it for the last 5 years or so.

There is much talk these days of the two forms of the Latin rite – the *forma ordinaria* and the *forma extraordinaria* – influencing each other. Frankly, I don't see how that influence can go in both directions; I can only see the older form bringing the newer form back into conformity with what the Church has taught for centuries. Although she was not discussing the liturgy per se in this quote, Muggeridge sums up the problem with this comment:

> Underlying the notion that if the Church debated longer there would be an end to religious crises is the very modern proposition that **truth is the end product of a dialectical process t**hat results in the unification of opposites into a truth transcending both, a concept **foreign** to Scripture's self-understanding, or to that of the Catholic Church at any time in its past. **The Church does not consider itself a debating society.** The rare general councils called when doctrinal confusion becomes intolerable "are not conferences where theologians beat out an understanding, a *modus vivendi*. They are assemblies where **authorized, or rather authoritative, witnesses testify to what the Church actually believes** on the point at issue." The intention is always, in the words of the Council of Trent, "to preserve the purity of the Gospel."

When the Church (after many years of arguing with him) announced in 1979 that Hans Küng was no longer to be considered a *Catholic* theologian, it was acting in a manner entirely consistent with its conception of its mission in history.

How can we ever reconcile a Mass where only the priest's hands touch the Body of Christ with a Mass where the man in the pew can do so?

How can we ever reconcile a Mass that is focused on God with one focused on man?

I doubt that the mind of the Church is amenable to such a compromise.

God, grant us more priests who see the truth, beauty, and splendor of the extraordinary form of the Mass. Grant us bishops willing to promote it. Grant that the eyes of the faithful are opened to its transcendent truth.

The Glass Ceiling Over the Traditional Latin Mass

So…you'd like your parish to offer the extraordinary form of the Mass. How do you get that to happen?

Fr. John Zuhlsdorf has addressed this basic question a few times on his own blog[45]. His standard answer is this (and it is a good one!):

> First, keep in mind that since *Summorum Pontificum* went into effect in September 2007 pastors of parishes, not diocesan bishops, implement celebrations of the Extraordinary Form in their parishes. The diocesan bishop no longer makes these decisions. Were a pastor of a parish to start a regular TLM, and were the diocesan bishop to demand that the priest stop, that priest's case would probably receive a very favorable hearing at the *Pontifical Commission "Ecclesia Dei"* (PCED) in Rome.

In other words, we look to the authoritative teachings and documents of the Church to determine the rights and responsibilities of both the laity and the clergy. In this case, there is a document – a *motu proprio* – entitled *Summorum Pontificum*, along with an instruction on that document called *Universae Ecclesiae*, which give a priest the right to say the EF Mass without obtaining the permission of the diocesan bishop. We also have the Pontifical Commission "Ecclesia Dei" in Rome, which has the authority to act on matters brought to its attention regarding problems and issues that the faithful may face in obtaining the EF Mass.

This is good, and is certainly understood by most of those who *support* access to the EF Mass. However, it is misconstrued and

---

[45] http://wdtprs.com/blog/

abused by those who do *not* support access to the EF Mass, including, sadly, a number of US bishops.

It's one thing for a priest to assert his right to provide the EF Mass for those faithful who desire it. It's another thing for him to actually accomplish the feat. If his bishop tells him to cease and desist from offering the Mass, a priest's most prudent choice is to obey that unfair and unlawful order. Why? Because, to put it bluntly, any priest doing something the bishop doesn't like, even if he is within his rights to do it, faces reprisals. There are plenty of examples out there.

Even if a priest decides to report the bishop's denial of the EF Mass to the PCED, the wheels turn slowly, I can tell you from experience. It doesn't appear to me that much is going on by way of fraternal correction in these matters. But then, one never knows what is going on behind the scenes. We can always hope.

There's another aspect to the stubborn (and unlawful) refusal of some bishops to allow parishes to provide the EF Mass. It is summed up nicely by a reader of Fr. Z's blog, which was quoted there[46] and appears here with Fr. Z's **emphases** and [*comments*]:

> We are struggling with our diocese over the definition of that term, as they [*"they"? Diocesan officials?*] want to say a stable group is **thirty Catholics** [*NO!*] who will pledge themselves to attend the EF. Naturally, we had numbers approaching thirty when our TLM was pushed out of the parishes three years ago. Now we total about fifteen or so, and even though the same people have attended the TLM more or less faithfully (we even found ourselves in a chapel

[46] http://wdtprs.com/blog/2011/12/quaeritur-how-to-get-gregorian-chant-and-a-tlm-in-the-parish/

of a secular retirement home for about two years) for four years, the diocese **still tells us we are not a stable group**. By the way, we had a priest in the area willing to offer this Mass for us. But the bishop banished him to the hinterlands. Now he travels about 300 miles once a month to offer this Mass for our group. **Just what *is* a "stable group"?**

A couple of tactics are evident here: first, the diocesan officials tell the group they don't have enough people to warrant an EF Mass. Second, in order to say that "it's just not possible" to provide the Mass for lack of a priest who is capable of saying it, the bishop moves the only available priest as far away as possible from the group that wants the EF Mass. Of course, the bishop will always be able to give a "good reason" why that particular priest had to be moved to Timbuktu.

Note that this can and does happen in any diocese. The bishop need only throw up his hands and say, "Sorry! No can do!" There are similar stories elsewhere (see the next chapter, "The Battle for the TLM").

So here you have an example of a diocese in which the EF is being effectively squelched. (And I am personally aware of well-documented squelching in at least two other dioceses, which I am not at liberty to discuss here.) This is a violation of the rights of the faithful, and it is an egregious and scandalous example of the disobedience of bishops to the authority of the Holy Father and the Church. And yet, it is often the "traditionalists", those people who want to "force Latin onto others", the ones who want to "turn back the clock", who are accused of infidelity to the Church.

Ironic, isn't it?

The Battle for the TLM: Conspiracy or Coincidence?

 An on-going battle in the Diocese of Little Rock, Arkansas, is reminiscent of the battle we have been fighting (and have mostly lost – for now) in the Diocese of Baker. It's the battle of the faithful to secure their right to have the extraordinary form of the Mass offered in their parishes. And in the end, it's the battle for the truths of the Catholic Church to be taught to the faithful.

In an article *in The Remnant*[47] (December 2011), author Ray Zürbeck pointed to numerous events in the Diocese – what he called "a long series of aggressive maneuvers" by Bishop Anthony Taylor – which had led to the demise of the Traditional Latin Mass in communities where it had been flourishing. One FSSP priest was dismissed from the diocese on grounds of "child abuse" (not sexual, and investigated and dropped by the local Department of Human Services). Another diocesan priest who had been saying the EF Mass regularly "was accused of some wrongdoing, and with no preliminary investigation he was removed from his position as pastor of St. Josephs in Fayetteville". Zürbeck maintains that the priest was "quickly cleared, but to this date his faculties have not been restored". And finally, a young priest (identified only as "Father X") who had been trained in Rome, understood *Summorum Pontificum*, and started offering an EF Mass received this treatment:

> …in late February 2010, Bishop Taylor personally escorted Father X to the St. Luke Institute in Silver Springs for "treatment" related to some supposed "personal problems." Every priest in the diocese knew exactly what those personal problems were – a desire to offer Mass in the Extraordinary Form.

---

[47] http://www.remnantnewspaper.com/Archives/2011-1225-zurbeck-bishop-taylor-father-demets.htm

Zürbeck summarizes the condition of the Diocese of Little Rock:

> And so, here we are in the year 2011 *Anno Domini,* with Catholics in Arkansas still having to fight for their right to the *Usus Antiquior* as if they were back in the 1970's.
> Bishop Taylor has found a way to get around *Summorum Pontificum*: **if a priest is caught praying in Latin, accuse him of some wrongdoing and broadcast it to the world.** It doesn't have to be true or accurate. Don't bother to investigate, just get it into the news media, destroy the man's reputation, and move on to the next target. It works! Even for good priests like Fathers Bradley and Demets. Or, better yet, send him to St. Luke's for "treatment." I'm guessing that Bishop Taylor and his henchmen will continue to purge the diocese of one holy priest after another in this manner. **What is there to stop them? It works!** At this point they are just a few steps away from accomplishing their mission, which seems to have everything to do with purifying the Diocese of Little Rock of **Catholic Tradition**. Catholic Tradition stands in the way of ideological agendas, you see.

Bishop Taylor responded to Zürbeck's challenges in another *Remnant* article[48] posted on February 13, 2012. He addresses many of the charges with lengthy explanations, and concludes:

> In any event, my purpose here is not to defend myself point by point against the allegations of Mr. Zürbeck, but simply to indicate that there is **no conspiracy in Arkansas against the Latin Mass and that there are in fact honorable reasons why I was forced to take each of the steps to which he ascribes such unworthy motives.** I am responsible for

---

[48] http://www.remnantnewspaper.com/Archives/2012-0215-bishop-taylor-responds.htm

protecting the flock entrusted to my care and for implementing the safe environment policies of the Church.

In a rebuttal following Bishop Taylor's explanation, Zürbeck maintains that there are still some facts that need to be addressed:

- One of the first things Bishop Taylor did when he arrived in Arkansas was to discontinue a newly-founded Latin Mass community in Berryville. This was **post** *Summorum Pontificum.*

- After leaving the people of Northwest Arkansas without a Latin Mass, Bishop Taylor publicly replied negatively to requests from the faithful that it be restored.

- Shortly after that, a young priest who began offering the Extraordinary Form of the Mass at odd hours during the week was admonished several times and then finally sent to St. Luke Institute. Since his return he no longer offers Mass in the Extraordinary Form.

And regarding the bishop's assurances that there is "no conspiracy" against the EF Mass, Zürbeck writes:

> Bishop Taylor states in his response: "*…. there are in fact honorable reasons why I was forced to take each of the steps to which he ascribes such unworthy motives.*" **Why are traditional Catholics in Arkansas seeing a hidden motive, then?** Well, the answer is simple: People find it odd that within the Diocese of Little Rock it seems that **something weird happens** to any diocesan priest who, on his own initiative**, begins offering a Latin Mass**.

So…how does all this relate to the Diocese of Baker? We saw a similar scenario – though on a smaller scale – develop when Bishop

Robert F. Vasa was transferred to the Diocese of Santa Rosa in early 2011, and a retired bishop was assigned as the Apostolic Administrator of the diocese.

Like Bishop Taylor in Arkansas, the Administrator of the Diocese of Baker made swift changes in the diocese that led to the complete disruption of an established EF Mass here. In short, the Administrator spuriously restricted the faculties of the priest who had been saying the EF Mass for our stable group; he moved two other priests who were able to say the EF Mass to the farthest corners of the diocese; and he encouraged another priest who had begun to say the EF Mass to reduce the frequency of these Masses (though the bishop did not insist on this). The Administrator also removed the tradition-sympathetic pastor of the parish where a monthly EF Mass had been held, and appointed instead a pastor who makes no secret of the fact that he "hates Latin" and has little sympathy for those "who try to shove Latin down our throats". It is unlikely that this priest will approve the use of the facilities for the EF Mass!

And the Administrator did all this while smiling to our faces and assuring us that he had nothing against the EF Mass – "in fact, we even have one of those in my diocese," he noted.

So, are all these little pieces of the puzzle just a coincidence? Come on. I took statistics in college…

I've been cautioned by a priest whom I respect that it is unwise to question a bishop's motives for moving priests, and that there may be reasons for the changes of which the laity is not made aware. I agree that this is a possibility. Still, my thought is that bishops seem to be pretty darn good at coming up with reasons that sound "pastoral", all the while using these "pastoral" decisions to further a rather *un*-pastoral program *against* the EF Mass.

And I have no doubt that some bishops *do* have such a program. Think about it: there seems to be little effort to make "pastoral" gestures toward the more tradition-minded members of the diocese! Until I start seeing diocesan websites that maintain a list of EF Masses available in their domain, and a training program for priests to learn the EF Mass, or at least *some* show of support for and promotion of the EF Mass, I will continue to doubt that there is widespread acceptance of and conformity to *Summorum Pontificum*. It ain't happenin' in Eastern Oregon, I can tell you that!

It's beyond credibility that the pattern of events taking place in dioceses all over this country is just a series of unhappy coincidences. I don't necessarily believe that there is a conscious, carefully-planned, cross-diocese conspiracy to keep the EF Mass under wraps, but…wait…could there be?!…Well, anyway, at the very least, there seems to be a certain mindset amongst some of the bishops which is preventing it from flourishing. And perhaps the bishops learn from each other the little techniques they can use to squelch the EF Mass without admitting that that is what they are doing.

For instance:

- It is well-known that seminarians – at least in certain dioceses and geographic areas – must keep any "traditionalist" tendencies they may have "under the radar" for fear of being dismissed on grounds of being "too rigid" or "not pastoral". (This has been a national problem for decades, and includes the whole issue of homosexuality in the priesthood, as well; see Michael S. Rose's book *Good-by, Good Men*.)

- Priests like Fr. Michael Rodriguez (El Paso, Texas) have been removed from their parishes and banished to the hinterlands, apparently for no better reason than that they were speaking the truth and/or offering the EF Mass. Fr. Rodriguez is not the only one, as Zürbeck's story and my own experiences have shown. I've heard similar stories now in Texas, Arkansas, Oregon, and Idaho…and that's without even looking for the problems.

- Even the laity comes under attack by bishops and/or diocesan "officials" for speaking the truth – Michael Voris and RealCatholicTV (now ChurchMilitant.TV), for example. There was also Daniel Avila, who dared to suggest that Satan might be involved in homosexuality, and lost his job as a result[49].

So we have hushing, shushing, and shuffling of priests and laity who take being Catholic quite seriously, who hold to Tradition, and who take care to preach and teach the Truth.

And all the while, "catholics" like Nancy Pelosi, Kathleen Sebelius, Joe Biden, and Sister Carol Keehan are allowed to continue to spread their heretical and scandalous thoughts to the detriment of the Church and the souls of the faithful, with barely a word of correction or condemnation of their false teaching.

Go figure.

If it's not a conspiracy of men, it is certainly a conspiracy of Satan and his minions.

---

[49] See http://philotheaonphire.blogspot.com/2011/11/devil-and-daniel-avila.html

Glimmers of Hope, Part 4

Blessed John XXIII Community in Lansing, Michigan

Here's some good news! It seems that Bishop Earl Boyea of the Diocese of Lansing, Michigan, has actually celebrated the extraordinary form of the Mass for a Latin Mass community in Lansing! More information about this interesting parish/community is available on their website "Get Holy"[50].

Blessed John XXIII Community[51] came into existence because the faithful were requesting the Traditional Latin Mass, says Fr. Jeffery Robideau, who serves as the chaplain of the group. Bishop Boyea asked priests to add the TLM in their parishes, but for whatever reasons, this didn't come to fruition. The bishop, aware that Fr. Robideau had a preference for the TLM, asked him to start a new community to meet the needs of the faithful who desired the older form of the Mass. Fr. Robideau's appointment took effect on Sept. 1, 2010 according to one news story[52].

Prior to that appointment, though, Fr. Robideau seems to have been put through the wringer in his previous parish. Fr. Z had a post about this[53] back in December 2009; he cited a news article about the situation which reported:

> Some 150 members of Our Lady of Fatima had asked Bishop Earl Boyea to remove the Rev. Jeffrey Robideau. Last week, the parish and diocese sent letters to parishioners saying that Robideau will stay.
>
> …
>
> Included in parishioners' concerns were Robideau's decision

---

[50]www.getholy.com
[51] http://www.getholy.com/BJ23.html
[52]http://www.mlive.com/news/jackson/index.ssf/2010/08/the_rev_jeffrey_robideau_to_le.html
[53]http://wdtprs.com/blog/2009/12/update-on-a-parish-conflict-in-michigan/

to **disband the church's choir** and his apparent **refusal to train girls** to perform altar services or hold church committee meetings.

"It is clear that the pastor has the prerogative to make the decisions in these matters," Boyea stated in his Dec. 17 letter. "You are no doubt aware that in our diocese, as in any diocese, priests will vary, within the guidelines established by universal or diocese law, in their choices in these matters."[54]

Sounds like Fr. Robideau had a clear idea about how to restore some true Catholic identity to his parish, and he actually had the support of his bishop in doing so! Wow! Kudos again to Bishop Boyea! And kudos to Fr. Robideau for standing up for his liturgical and pastoral rights in the first place!

So now, Fr. Robideau is the chaplain for Blessed John XXIII Community in Lansing, Michigan. The extraordinary form of the Mass is celebrated in the crypt of the Cathedral every Sunday, with anywhere from 50-80 people in attendance. This is generally a low Mass, with a missa cantata (sung Mass) on the first Sunday of the month. Fr. Robideau says that the group does have a schola, and plans are in the works to have a sung Mass on two Sundays per month. Easter Sunday marked the group's first solemn high Mass. (There are also two weekday Masses, one in the evening and one in the morning.)

And, as I mentioned above, Bishop Boyea himself has celebrated the EF Mass for this group. That, to me, is significant.

There are two main pages on the "Get Holy" website; one describes "Saintly Acres", which is a 20-acre farm where Fr. Robideau lives

---

[54] http://www.mlive.com/news/jackson/index.ssf/2009/12/catholic_bishop_ says_priest_wi.html

and also conducts short retreats for his parishioners. The "About Us"[55] section says:

> The name Get Holy represents the heart of our spiritual life. We are to "Get Holy." That is to say, we are to know, love and serve God. We are to transform our lives into the image of the Body of Christ. We are to conquer our personal interior disordered passions and desires known as concupiscence.
>
> Those who want to Get Holy must use a different approach than the one most of the world uses, including most clerics. We are not to take the road of least resistance. Rather, we ask what is the will of God and then we are to take that road whether it be easy or difficult. This is done with the understanding that people will rise to the level of excellence demanded of them. We are not called to water down the Faith, but to present it in all its fullness for the glory of God and the salvation of souls.
>
> At Saintly Acres, we are dedicated to the tried and true methods of growing in holiness as lived by the many great saints in our rich history.
>
> We look for and demand nothing less than the fulfillment of Jesus' command "Be ye perfect as your heavenly Father is perfect."
>
> We are here for you.

Fr. Robideau seems to be a no-holds-barred kind of priest when it comes to preaching. In the "News and Articles"[56] section, he posts

---

[55] http://www.getholy.com/About_Us.html
[56] http://getholy.com/blog/

sermons; the ones I looked through seemed to have solid, honest, no-nonsense Church teaching. When I commented on this in an email to Fr. Robideau, he responded, "Jesus never held back so I figure why should I, as long as I speak truth of faith and not from opinion."

The other main page of the website is devoted to Blessed John XIII Community. I like the section that says:

> Are you nervous about going to your first Extraordinary Form Mass?
>
> Don't be. We have a Pew Buddy for you.
>
> We are more than happy to help you. We have people willing to sit with you and help you follow along in our Latin/English books so you know exactly what is going on.
>
> We all remember our first time. It is an exciting time so forget being nervous and come and be spiritually enrichened through this ancient rite of the Catholic Mass.

I haven't been to Lansing to experience all of this first hand, but I find it very encouraging to know that there are groups of the faithful who want this to happen, that there are priests like Fr. Robideau willing to serve the faithful in this way, and that there are bishops like Bishop Boyea who actually seem to support it.

That's a far cry from the situation in my diocese, but it gives me hope!

The Traditional Latin Mass in Oregon

Although we're not having much success in re-instituting the extraordinary form of the Mass here in the Diocese of Baker, I'm taking some encouragement from recent developments in the neighboring Archdiocese of Portland. Here are two different stories that are both worth jumping up and down about!

First story: I was made aware that the celebration of the extraordinary form of the Mass was planned in Southern Oregon, via the "Orate Fratres" blog, which had this announcement:

> It's confirmed… What was previously known as the Tridentine Mass, or Traditional Latin Mass, and most recently, the "extraordinary form" of the Mass, will be *periodically* offered to worshipers at Our Lady of the River Catholic Church in Rogue River, Oregon.[57]

And the first such Mass did happen on February 10, 2013. One attendee told me that several years ago a petition had been made to have the EF Mass offered in their area, but – the typical story – they were stonewalled because the powers-that-be said there "wasn't any interest". Ha! As she commented to me in an email, "Last night's Mass, with 150 in attendance and standing room only at Our Lady of the River seems to indicate otherwise!"

Second story: In other good news for the tradition-minded in Oregon, a correspondent alerted me to a wonderful letter by Fr. J. Michael Morrissey, pastor of St. Catherine of Siena parish in Veneta, Oregon. Veneta is also home to an SSPX chapel (St. Thomas Becket); from the letter, you can tell see that Fr. Morrissey understands the implications of that for the faithful of his parish who desire the TLM.

I've pasted in the entire letter below, but I'd like to point out a few things about the spirit that shines through that letter (to me, at least).

---

[57] http://fratres.wordpress.com/2013/01/01/extraordinary-form-coming-to-southern-oregon/

1. Fr. Morrissey wants to conform to Pope Benedict XVI's wishes concerning the Mass.
2. He does not see the extraordinary form of the Mass as a threat.
3. He recognizes the needs of the faithful and is trying to meet them.
4. He wants to form "a stable community of people whose desire for this form of the Liturgy. He WANTS it to happen. He's not just waiting for "enough people" to say they want it.
5. He's asking people change! He's asking for an adjustment to the Mass schedule!

This letter epitomizes what I would love to see coming from *bishops*! I don't know Fr. Morrissey, but I have written him a letter thanking him for what he is attempting to do. He gives me hope!

Here's the letter in its entirety with my **emphases**:

February 2013

Dear Fellow Catholics,

My name is Fr. J. Michael Morrissey and I am Pastor of St Catherine of Siena in Veneta. I am about to begin my second term of office in Veneta and my 35th year of priesthood. With two short periods of time off I have been a pastor almost continuously for over 32 years. Much of that experience has been in parishes of diverse language needs.

The Liturgy of the Church has long been one of my deepest loves and it was with a joyful heart that I have tried to **receive the guidance of Pope Benedict** *to undertake a "reform of the reform" of the Liturgy of the Roman Rite. Indeed over the years I have consciously tried to* *bring the graces of that effort to my ministry here at St Catherine of Siena.*

These efforts are bearing fruit and I believe they are about to enter upon a new phase under the guidance of the Holy Spirit. By God's grace the time has come for a renewed effort in this parish to **address the needs** *of the many Catholics among us who prefer what Pope Benedict calls the* **Extraordinary Form of the Latin Rite–** *using the liturgical books of 1962 to celebrate what is popularly known as the Tridentine Rite.*

Over the past few years in the Eugene area vicariate, **sporadic efforts** *have been made to make a Mass in the Extraordinary Form available but, in* **my personal judgment, all these efforts have suffered from the planned lack of consistency** *and the lack of local priests willing and able to provide the Mass on a regular, stable basis.* **That needs to change***.*

After much prayer, reflection and extensive conversation with the leadership of St
Catherine I have concluded that in my second term of office a renewed and serious effort should be made. I do not envision the provision of a Latin Mass on an on again, off again basis, but rather **an enduring commitment to the formation of a stable community of people whose desire for this form of the Liturgy has gone unfulfilled for too long***. This vision is quite different from prior efforts.*

Because I had just started High School when the Ordinary Form was introduced, I have no prior experience as a priest celebrant of the Extraordinary Form. I am not completely unfamiliar in that I had served the Mass for years on a daily basis and enjoyed my extensive studies of the Latin language in the seminary. **Now I have begun to** *take the steps necessary to be trained in the rubrics of the Extraordinary Form so that I can make it available.*

*Having waited in vain for the return to full communion and canonical status of the SSPX so that we might legitimately reap the benefits of their presence among us, over the past year the Pastoral Council of the parish has extensively discussed and unanimously decided that we so want the graces to be gained from this opportunity that **we are willing to ask the folks attending St Catherine to make a major adjustment** to the Mass schedule of the parish in order to accommodate a new EF Mass at Noon every Sunday. It means the cancellation of an English Mass and the consolidation of all our folks into one Sunday Mass. That is asking a lot of them.*

Obviously this effort calls for sacrifices to be made. Despite the poor health which occasioned my assignment to the parish, I am willing to dedicate the considerable time and energy that will be needed and the parish leadership is willing to lead our folks through a major adjustment in order to make it happen. We do this without knowing how you might respond and in the sincere hope that the response will be favorable.

We hope you will give us the chance and the support needed to make this effort a success.

At this time we anticipate that we can be ready to begin offering Mass in Latin at noon every Sunday starting no later than the first Sunday in June 2013. In the meantime we have sought to gather anyone willing to help us get mobilized to lend a hand by attending Organizational Meetings planned for Feb 16, Mar 23, and April 13 at 10 am in the Parish Hall. Please consider joining us.

Your prayers for the success of this effort are most certainly needed.

Sincerely in Christus Dominus,

Fr. J. Michael Morrissey
Pastor, St. Catherine of Siena, Veneta

Section VI:

Dealing With It

Since the Passover of the Jews was near, Jesus went up to Jerusalem. He found in the temple area those who sold oxen, sheep, and doves, as well as the money-changers seated there. He made a whip out of cords and drove them all out of the temple area, with the sheep and oxen, and spilled the coins of the money-changers and overturned their tables, and to those who sold doves he said, "Take these out of here, and stop making my Father's house a marketplace."

His disciples recalled the words of scripture, "Zeal for your house will consume me.

John 2: 13-17

Suffering Through Mass

Sometimes bad liturgy happens to good people. That is, sometimes the faithful who desire to experience a liturgically correct Mass are denied the opportunity. What options are available when such a situation exists in one's parish?

Of course, one could respectfully ask the pastor to address and correct the abuses… [crickets chirping]. Yeah, right. Speaking from my own experience, I can say that this approach is not often successful.

Another option is to "jump ship" to a different parish where the Mass is celebrated in a more liturgically correct manner. This can be a prudent decision; after all, *lex orandi, lex credenda*: as we pray, so we believe. Bad liturgy can affect one's faith – and especially the faith of one's children.

But…what happens when your choices are limited? I mean *seriously limited*, as they are where I live in Eastern Oregon. Parishes are few and far between, out here in the wild West; only two cities in our entire diocese have more than one parish. Very few parishes have a Mass that reflects even a modicum of tradition. It's not that there are clown Masses or dancing girls in every parish; no, I don't think either of those abominations can be found here. But the parishes in my diocese, in my experience, are undeniably and unashamedly…*mediocre.* They are lukewarm, at best.

I haven't been to every parish in the diocese; I haven't even been to many! But I have talked to people who attend at different parishes, and have heard the stories. I also know a couple of priests who have traveled extensively in the diocese; they have visited most of the parishes and celebrated Mass there, and they know the other priests. I asked one priest the following questions about the state of the liturgy in this diocese; his smart-alecky responses are in *italics*:

Do you know of any parish in our Diocese where Gregorian chant is sung on even a semi-regular basis?

> *What's "Gregorian chant"?*

Do you know of any parish where Latin is used regularly, even for just a part of the (Sunday) Mass?

> *Didn't the Church get rid of Latin at Vatican II?*

How many/which parishes have only male altar servers?

> *How sexist!* [Actually, I know of two parishes where the priest has taken action to ensure that only males will serve.]

Which parish of the Diocese has the most liturgically correct Mass, in your experience?

> *Probably least egregious:* [He named a parish which I will leave unnamed; but note that he uses the phrase "least egregious" – rather than "best"]

Even if my priest friend could name a parish that was "acceptable", odds are it would be too far away from my home for weekly travel. The parish that probably has the most liturgical correctness and the most appropriately-appointed sanctuary is an hour-and-a-half drive from us, and in winter that includes driving over two of the most dangerous mountain passes in the state!

So, what do we do when our liturgical options are so seriously curtailed?

I have a suggestion, especially for those who want a TLM but have no access to one, but also for *Novus Ordo* aficionados who are tired of guitars, tambourines, and adlibbed prayers. The suggestion comes from a correspondent, but these are my thoughts and actions exactly:

> Go to Mass at your current parish, wear your chapel veil, bring your 1962 Missal with you, and **pray from your missal** throughout the Mass in **reparation** for the sins of the world and the **dishonor to God of this and so many other Masses**. The Missal will serve the purpose of occupying your mind, your hands and your eyes. You can skip Holy Communion and make a spiritual communion instead.
>
> In other words, you won't have to watch what is going on, you won't have to get involved in all the "hand stuff", and your mind can focus on the prayers of the Mass in your Missal. In this way you are honoring God in multiple ways, including obedience: you are praying, you are actually participating in the Mass in a deeper way than those around you, and your suffering has merit and means something!

I also avoid the "sign of peace" as much as possible, finding it a distraction and an interruption of the "flow" of the rubrics and prayers of the Mass. Having a missal in my hands and looking at it throughout the handshaking phase of Mass is an effective way of saying, "It's not that I don't like you; I'm just busy praying."

My correspondent adds:

> You may choose to receive Holy Communion or you may not, depending on a whole variety of factors. The point of this method of participation at Mass is that you are "keeping

holy the Lord's day" in **the only public way available to you**. You are **giving witness** to the priest and those around you by participating quietly (and one priest says this makes priests uneasy, and that it's good for them!). The important thing is to not let what is going on around you "disturb your peace." **If you were at Calvary, your participation would be silent and filled with grief.** You are simply declining to participate in the event of Calvary in a wholly inappropriate way. You are choosing to suffer **for** Our Lord, in obedience.

Who knows? Such **silent but public acts of reparation** may have the same effect that the Carmelites of Compiegne had on the French Revolution: you will effect change through your suffering that could not be accomplished in any other way.

This is a good answer to "what do we do now?" – when there is no other parish nearby that is leading you to holiness. Everyone can do this in their current parish, no matter how bad it is. Imagine the effect on an errant priest if a sizable portion of the congregation stopped chit-chatting before and after Mass, stopped glad-handing each other at the sign of peace, and stopped singing the inane ditties offered as liturgical music!

But even more than that, imagine the effect of those actions on your own soul. You will be "actively (actually) participating" in Mass in the way intended by the Church. Imagine how pleasing to God your actions will be as you join your suffering to that of His Son on the Cross

After all, it's really about the Cross, isn't it? And we much each bear our own, even if that includes bad liturgy.

Feel the Pain

In the comment section of one post on my blog, some of us got to commiserating about the state of liturgical affairs in our various parishes and in the Church as a whole.

Now, we all know that things can be really, really, really bad – like clown Masses and beer tent Masses, and bishops high-fiving each other and holding balloons at Mass – or they can be "sorta-kinda bad", with bad homilies, adlibbing of prayers, lay ministers in shorts and flip-flops, etc… and all gradations in between. Sadly, we hear few reports about parishes that have liturgies where the rubrics are faithfully followed, and where there is liturgically correct music as well!

Those who desire truly reverent and correct liturgical worship do experience pain at Masses that fall short in the rubrics department. And many have found that the Masses that *don't* fall short are the ones offered in the extraordinary form, AKA the Traditional Latin Mass. Funny how that works.

Here are a few comments from the post mentioned above:

> The final straw in my parish church occurred on Sunday. I have been hanging on by a frayed string for some time now there, but Sunday's "homily" on the sin of "individualism", building the Reign of God on earth, and the priesthood of the people did me in. It is often a straw that breaks the camel's back. But [it was] the conversation between the priest and an EM in front of the open tabernacle that caused me the most pain. As an afterthought, the priest made a reluctant bow, and the EM thought to imitate him and do the same as they hurried away.

As I think I already mentioned here, I am a former sedevacantist/SSPX chapel goer. That is where I am on the brink of returning - to my sedevacantist chapel. Our diocese is bad....

...I have been advised to sit home, but I cannot do that. **I just want a place where I have my faith and a reverent Mass**.

Another commenter lamented:

I am struggling right now. I have people telling me I need to go to the NO Mass...but I can hardly stand to be there after 3 years of the diocesan TLM only. This difference is wearing on me and the children.

Lately, I began going to the local SSPX chapel for First Fridays only and have found such an oasis there that I want to keep going back...

I often wonder why it is that the people who just want a liturgy that's celebrated according to the rubrics and according to the various documents of the Church – even the Vatican II documents! – are ignored, at best; and at worst they are ostracized, ridiculed, and otherwise brow-beaten. The minute a pastor makes a change in the liturgically correct direction, a handful of "progressive" voices protest and say they'll leave the parish if they don't get their way. And the pastor waffles. Why is that?!

Whatever the reason, that's the way it is. Of course, we should still respectfully make known our desire for a properly celebrated Mass – it's our right to have a decent liturgy (see "A Liturgical Bill of Rights", p. 27), and it's even a duty to bring to pastors' attention the abuses we observe. However, I suspect we will have to endure bad liturgy for some years to come.

Yet another commenter mentioned and provided a link to an article by Fr. John Hardon entitled "How to Cope with Abuses in the Eucharistic Liturgy"[58]. I'll give you a few excerpts here with a few comments interspersed (my **emphases** throughout), but I recommend reading the entire article.

Fr. Hardon notes from the outset that "[f]rom the very beginning of the Church's existence Catholics have been obliged to assist at Mass every Sunday and at…Days of Obligation", and that Catholics are well aware of this.

> Catholics commonly recognize the seriousness of their duty. As a result, their **conscience** tells them to participate in the Holy Sacrifice… This same conscience is **now being tested** in not a few cases to the breaking point because of the **widespread liturgical abuses** going on throughout the United States as well as other countries in the Western world.

> Basically our question is, how does a Catholic satisfy this grave duty of assisting at Mass…on Sundays and days of Obligation where the Holy Sacrifice of the Mass is offered in ways that are frequently, **very often nothing less than scandalous to the faithful**?

Fr. Hardon gives us an example of a hypothetical parish

> …[L]et us suppose we are members of Ethel Rita Parish, located in the town of Middleburg. Our pastor and the only priest of the parish is Fr. Filbert Imbecilius who introduced altar girls many years ago. He refuses to distribute Holy Communion to anyone kneeling. Either you are standing for Holy Communion or he will pass you by.

---

[58] http://www.therealpresence.org/archives/Mass/Mass_004.htm

Fr. Filbert regularly omits the Gloria and substitutes what he calls the "Prayer of Belief." He never says the Nicene Creed. He changes the wording of both the Sacramentary and the Lectionary to eliminate every even suggestion of sexist language. He uses strange looking and even stranger tasting altar bread. Regularly he refers to God as Father, Mother or pronouns He or She. He insists that everyone stand for the whole Eucharistic Prayer. He regularly changes the words of the Mass, including the words of consecration, to suit his own fancy. He hardly ever celebrates Mass without a crowd of what he calls facilitators. Most of whom are well known as zealous feminists who join their hands around the altar during the Eucharistic Prayer.

Fr. Hardon goes on in a way that would be humorous, were it not so true! And he notes too, that in this hypothetical parish:

Countless letters, letters of complaint, have been sent to the Bishop of the diocese. Every letter **has gone unanswered**, and there is no reason to expect that the Bishop will make any effort to change the abuses in this parish. In fact, the only occasion when the Bishop made any public statement on the subject of the liturgy was when **he rejected a petition to allow the celebration of the Tridentine Mass** in his diocese. Said the Bishop, "There is no need to return to the past." and the **petitioners were labeled, "Liturgical Reactionaries"** by his Holy Excellency.

Sound familiar?! Then Fr. Hardon addresses the problem of the distance one must travel to attend a Mass "celebrated with some regard for the lawful norms" – again addressing a concern many of us face. He also addresses the remedy some have found:

A few years ago some members of St. Ethel Rita became so disgusted that they formed a private liturgical association, and now hold meetings every other Sunday in an old Protestant church building which they have purchased and converted into a small parish. These meetings are followed by a Tridentine Mass celebrated, of course, without the permission of the Bishop of Middleburg.

Fr. Hardon also addresses the canonical considerations involved in attending an SSPX Mass. He notes:

> In my judgment, Catholics do fulfill their duty of assisting at Sunday Mass by attending in the Holy Sacrifice a church affiliated with those who are members with a schismatic group like the Lefebvres. But then I also must add that the Catholics be sure that those seeing them attending these schismatic Masses are not scandalized into thinking that professed Roman Catholics have given up their fidelity to the Bishop of Rome.

Unfortunately, many *do* assume that anyone who attends an SSPX Mass no longer maintains "fidelity to the Bishop of Rome". Perhaps they can be educated!

In order to cope with the abuses of the liturgy, Fr. Hardon suggests that the faithful must increase their understanding of the Eucharist, noting that there has been an unfortunate abundance of wrong theology about the Eucharist, with

> …books [that] teach widely …that the **Eucharist is essentially the gathering of the faithful**…

> They will tell you a priest **saying Mass alone is not offering the Eucharistic Sacrifice**. What we are calling liturgical abuses are only symptoms of deep doctrinal errors that have penetrated once Catholic circles and are causing **untold damage to the faith**, and I mean it, of millions!

...So many people nowadays are speaking about **Eucharistic celebration**. So few are ever talking about the **Sacrifice of the Mass**... [T]here is no substitute for understanding the Holy Eucharist as the Sacrifice of the Mass which is, we believe, a representation of Christ's sacrifice on Calvary.

...The main reason for the loss of millions of once believing Catholics is they **have not understood what they have believed**. Either you understand the meaning of the Holy Eucharist or in today's world you will **cease to remain** a Catholic.

Fr. Hardon also suggests that it is extremely important to

...keep up to date [with] the Church's directives on how the Holy Eucharist is to be celebrated, worshipped and received. And hear it, the **final arbiter** on the Holy Eucharist is not, is not, the **Bishop of the diocese. It is the Bishop of Rome.**

Fr. Hardon's third means of coping with liturgical abuse is "prudential courage". He says:

We must be courageous, and I mean **courageous in professing our faith in Jesus Christ present in the Blessed Sacrament and offering Himself in the Sacrifice of the Mas**s in today's world and what I am saying refers not only to the laity but also and with painful emphasis to priests.

...The Catholic Church will survive **only** where there are still bishops, priests, and the laity who have the **supernatural, even heroic, fortitude** to live up to what they know the Vicar of Christ expects of those who call themselves Catholics.

There is much more to this article, so please go and read it! And keep in mind this prayer Fr. Hardon offers at the end of the conference:

> Lord Jesus, we beg you to give us the strength to not just believe internally in your Real Presence in the Blessed Sacrament. Give us the strength to profess our faith, especially in the company of people who have accepted widespread Eucharistic liturgical abuses and consider us out of touch with the times.

> Mary our Mother, ask your Son to make us strong in following Him really present in the Blessed Sacrament even if this would cost us our lives. Amen.

Glimmers of Hope: Dealing with Despair Over the State of the Church

I stumbled upon a homily by Fr. Chad Ripperger[59] of the FSSP. He makes some very good points about the reactions "traditionalists" might have to the liturgical abuses and lack of catechesis, etc., they see in the Church. For instance, he notes:

> …[I]t's very easy for traditionalists, I think, to become depressed, or to suffer despair, because they see by the grace of God, no less, all the problems within the Church. And yet, we must be very careful that when we see how bad everything is that we do not judge things by excess.

> …[I]f we have a passion in relationship to these things, that passion drags us to excess or defect in our judgment. And so we have to be very careful not to let sorrow overtake our judgment of how bad everything is – in the sense of looking at things and saying that we're all doomed, or suffering from despair.

> Sometimes, because of how bad things are, traditionalists will allow anger to consume their life by viewing the Church. That is, every time they think of the Church, they get angry at the things that various people do within the Church. We have to be very careful to not allow the problems in the Church to affect our spiritual life.

I found his words very helpful, as I do at times find myself falling into a bit of despair over the state of the Church. And I do experience that anger he's talking about as well!

---

[59] See Fr. Ripperger's website at http://www.sensustraditionis.org/

Fr. Ripperger emphasizes that our ability to see the problems in the Church comes only from the grace of God. He points out that our suffering is real, but that we must strive to maintain humility and charity in our reactions to that suffering and those who cause it by their actions in the Church.

You can listen to the entire homily (about 13 minutes) online[60]. I present my transcription of the homily below. I apologize to Fr. Ripperger in advance for any errors; in some places I have edited the actual spoken words slightly for ease in reading. All **emphases** are mine.

** ** ** ** **

"Do not let the sun go down on your anger, do not give place to the devil." In the name of the Father and the Son and the Holy Ghost. Amen.

As traditionalists, we have to be very careful never to go to excess or defect in our reactions to things like the state of the Church, to what people say, things of this sort. And there are certain excesses and defects, which as traditionalists, it's very easy for us to fall into. And so we must constantly be on guard against them. For, of course, **virtue lies in the mean between excess and defect**, but even more so, we want to know what the truth is and to lead a life according to that truth in a perfect manner.

And so I think it would be good for us to take a look at the defects which traditionalists very often suffer, to just see whether we have these defects; and if so, take the means to avoid them. There are a number of them, but I think we'll just stick with a few.

The first is that it's very easy for traditionalists, I think, to **become depressed**, or to **suffer despair**, because they see by the grace of

---

[60] http://www.sensustraditionis.org/webaudio/Sermons/Disk2/Problems.mp3

God, no less, all the problems within the Church. And yet, we must be very careful that when we see how bad everything is, that we do not judge things by excess. So, for instance, sometimes you'll see traditionalists – not all of them, not the faithful ones, of course, but some of them who argue that the *Novus Ordo* Mass is invalid, or that there is no Pope, for instance with the sedevacantists.

But we all know that it's very easy when we see these things that are bad, to judge by excess. St. Thomas tells us that when we judge things intellectually, we judge things based with what we see in our imagination, that is, what we experience. And so **if we have a passion** in relationship to these things, that passion drags us to excess or defect in our judgment. And so we have to be very careful **not to let sorrow overtake our judgment of how bad everything is** – in the sense of looking at things and saying that we're all doomed, or suffering from despair.

Sometimes because of how bad things are, traditionalists will **allow anger to consume their life** by viewing the Church. That is, every time they think of the Church, they get angry at the things that various people do within the Church. We have to be very careful to not allow the problems in the Church to affect our spiritual life. If these problems begin to cause us to, for instance, detract against the members of the Magisterium or things like this, then we have to be very careful that if we see that, that we do what is necessary in order to put an end to it.

Now very often, what that means is that if we start seeing things are so bad, we have to **get our mind off of it for a while** just so that we don't end up being drawn into this **excess of being angry** and end up doing things that we should not. Now that **doesn't mean that we're ignorant** of the situation; it doesn't mean you put blinders on. It just means that when you see some defect in the Church that you should see that as God revealing it to you because **He gives you the grace**

to see it, so that you can recognize it and then **do something about it**, that is to **pray for those who cause the problem**.

We also need to have a **detachment** even from the idea of a healthy Church – even though we must strive for the Church to be healthy. In other words, the Church is our means to God, and so when we see members of the Church who are spiritually dysfunctional, let us put it that way, or just disordered, we have to be very careful **not to let that distract us from growing in holiness**, and so we should seek a certain detachment from the members, that is from seeing things in perfect order. Not that we shouldn't strive for it, but that **if God wants us to suffer it**, we accept it **in humility**.

We must also be **detached from vindication**. St. Thomas says that anger is a complex passion. That is, we have a certain sorrow, we suffer some harm, or we're afflicted with some harm, which all of us are by virtue of this state of the Church; and so, from that anger can arise [a situation] in which we seek the vindication of the harm that's been caused to us. In that particular case we have to be careful that we have a detachment from the desire for vindication. We have to recognize that **in the end, God will straighten it out, and every person will pay the last farthing**.

We have to be sure that the problems in the Church do not affect our charity. If it does, then we have to, again, get our minds off of it.

We also have to be careful about detracting against the Magisterium. Now, the moralists say that we can say something negative or say something that takes away from someone's reputation only if there are **three conditions** that are met. The first is that it proceeds from charity, that you should do it for the love of God – not for the love of vindication, not for the love of getting your appetite sated – but out of **true charity**. That is, it's being done **for the sake of a person who has the defect**.

Second, it has to be **just**. We don't exaggerate it, we don't diminish it; we say it precisely to the degree that is necessary. Which brings up the third one: it has to be **necessary**. We have to be very careful in getting together and gossiping and complaining about the state of the Church and the various members of the Church to sate our own desire, that is vindication; or sate our own desires to see their reputation lessened in some way. Rather we have to only speak about these things when it's necessary, **either for our salvation or for the spiritual well-being of someone else**. And we have to be very careful about this detraction because very often people will detract against members of the Magisterium, meanwhile committing the **sin of omission for not praying** for the priests, bishops, and the pope who may have these defects.

We must also be careful **not to allow our filial devotion** to the office of the Papacy **to wane**. Now, clearly you have to make a distinction between the man who might occupy that office, and the office itself. Even St. Peter had defects; that's clear in the Gospels. But that doesn't detract from the fact that he's still the Pope; he has an awesome responsibility, and therefore we must pray for him. And if we find that we start getting to the point where we don't even want to look at him, we don't even want to listen to him, we don't even want to hear him, then in that particular case we need to start **working on our charity** and **start praying** for him.

We cannot give in also to the **vice of curiosity**. Sometimes, traditionalists know there's a problem and they want to understand the problem better, which is a legitimate desire; but sometimes, it gives way to a type of curiosity in which one just constantly goes around **seeking to find out everything that's wrong** because you're **suffering** from what they're doing and so you want to see everything that they're doing wrong so that you feel nice about it. You have to be very careful about this because this type of curiosity can destroy our faith if we're not careful. And it can also **affect us**

psychologically and spiritually, which is **clearly demonic**, because the **demons will use the defects in the Church in order to distract us from advancing in our spiritual life.**

We have an obligation **to protect our faith** and sometimes that even means avoiding people who tell us the truth, for which we are unprepared psychologically, spiritually, and intellectually. In other words, if we know, in reading a book, that it's going to end up affecting our faith or end up [hurting] our spiritual life, then we have to avoid it. Period. Not because of the truth that's involved – we don't avoid the truth as such – but **because of our own state.**

Again while we have to be aware of the problems of the Church, I don't think you have to read a whole lot to be aware of it. If God's given you the grace to see the problems, it's a good thing to read knowledgeable priests who understand the situation and will proceed according to charity and truth, and present the problem clearly, than to read people who are very acrimonious about the state of the Church.

We must also be careful because sometimes this curiosity will end up burning up the time that should be spent **reading the saints**, or **educating ourselves in the faith.** It is too easy to get wrapped up in the problems in the Church, rather than just instruct ourselves in the faith. That's why I don't personally spend a whole lot of time reading books about the state of the Church. I already know what the problems are, usually better than the author does. And that's the reason I don't spend too much time. But from time to time, it's necessary for the priest to be knowledgeable about these things, so he can tell people whether it's a good book or not. But at the same time, as a priest myself, and also you as laymen, **your obligation is to know the faith, not to know the problems** - even though that's necessary to avoid losing your faith. But your **principle obligation is to educate yourself** in your faith, and if these things are going to detract from that obligation, then you have to put them aside. So the point is, read books that teach you more about the faith, not what just tell you all the problems.

We can also see a bit of a problem because traditionalists are hurt or because they want to see the truth, and because they have a love for the truth and for what the Church teaches, they will very often engage in argumentation which we are not intellectually prepared for out of a desire to defend what we know is true. Now we have to careful about this. Obviously, we have an obligation to defend the truth according to prudence, of course; we don't defend it in every circumstance because sometimes that'll actually cause things to be worse. But at the same time, we have to defend the truth to the degree that we are able, but if we start recognizing that we're getting a bit in over our head, we have to kind of step back and ask somebody who knows better to engage in that argumentation.

I'll give you an example of this. There was a case of an article that recently appeared on a website that talked about homophobia, and it gave an etymology of the term homophobia saying "homo" came from man and phobia came from fear. The person didn't even know what they were talking about. "Homo" is the Latin derivation, not the Greek, and psychological terms are in Greek, so the "homo" means "same" - it's fear of homosexuals. The person got it completely wrong. And so I got to the first line and recognized this person doesn't know what they're talking about, so I just didn't even finish reading the article. So the point is that you have to be very careful, and I see this a bit more with laity more than – and even priests, because you see this even with priests, but more so with laity who...they'll take the time very often to research the subject, for instance some aspect of ecclesiology or something like that, but very often they're unaware of a broader understanding of it and so they make rather egregious problems.

So what does this mean? It means that we have to **defend the faith** but we're only obligated to defend the faith **to the degree of our ability**. And we should know that limitation and not go beyond it.

We have to be sure that we do not always seek to **beat people over the head with the truth**, either – for example, about the state of the Church. Granted, we're **suffering**, very often at the very hands of the people we're supposed to be charitable to, but … just because God gave us a grace to see the problem, that doesn't give us license to beat people over the head who can't see it. **We must accept that some people simply aren't going to get it, because they do not have the grace**. Or that, when we see that they don't get it, we have to engage in some type of prayer, fasting, or mortification, or some type of good works so that **we can merit the grace for them** to see it.

We also have to be very careful about when we're able to see it because of the grace which comes from God. We have to be careful that this doesn't provide an ego trip for us – that somehow, we're better, that we know this; other people don't know it, we're just the elite, we're just much better. The fact that God gives you the grace to see it – because **nobody can see it without God's grace** – is a sign **it didn't come from you** so there is no foundation for you being proud. Rather what it is, is God showing you the problem. And so, as a result, because it comes from grace, we are humbled at the fact that we're so blind that we can't see it without God giving us the grace.

And so, **what do we have to do?** If we're going to approach the situation in the Church and to help people, and to be the best thing that we can for the state of the Church, **we have to grow in holiness**. But we have to also be **meek**, so that we don't become angry; we have to have a certain **humility** so that we're not proud; we have to have a certain **charity** so we don't abuse people; but at the same time we have to beg God for **the fortitude to struggle against the**

disastrous state of the Church so that it **doesn't affect our faith,** and so that we can be **faithful to Him to the end**…In the name of the Father and of the Son and of the Holy Ghost, amen.

EPILOGUE

Hope Springs Eternal

I am not a Bible scholar by any means, but it seems to me that we may find a source of solace and hope in the books of Ezra and Nehemiah, where the story is told of the rebuilding of the temple at Jerusalem. In a sense, those who are struggling against "bad liturgy" and fighting to reinstate the extraordinary form of the Mass are attempting to rebuild the "temple" that is our Faith. The Eucharist is, after all, the source and summit of our faith[61], and when the celebration of Mass is deficient, it can only lead to a deficient faith. Many writers and speakers have noted the truth of this statement: the increase in abuses of the liturgy, especially in the *Novus Ordo*, certainly seems to correlate with a decline in the markers of a robust faith, such as vocations to the priesthood and religious life, attendance at Mass by the lay faithful, and fidelity to the teachings of the Church by bishops, priests, and laity.

In the book of Ezra, we see the beginning of the account of the rebuilding of the temple at Jerusalem. The reigning non-Jewish monarch, King Cyrus, actually commanded it, and the Israelites began the work in good faith. Soon, however, naysayers undermined the project; first, they offered to join in and help, saying "for we seek your God just as you do" (Ezra 4:2). They were only seeking to undermine the project from within, though; and when the Israelites declined their help, the Samaritans then "set out to intimidate and dishearten the people of Judah so as to keep them from building. They also suborned counselors to work against them and thwart their plans" (Ezra 4:5). Finally, the enemies of the Jews succeeded in persuading a later king to put a halt to the rebuilding.

Years went by with no work being done, but it would seem that the Israelites did not give up hope; they finally began to build again when some bold Israelites listened to the words of their prophets.

---

[61] *Lumen Gentium,* 11

When questioned by the local authorities, they insisted on their right to rebuild, and noted that a previous king had given permission; after a review of the past documents, the reigning monarch allowed them to proceed. Then, in the book of Nehemiah, we are told of the rebuilding of Jerusalem's walls. Still the naysayers were fighting against the completion of the work; Nehemiah himself cries out, "Take note, O our God, how we were mocked! Turn back their derision on their own heads and let them be carried away to a land of captivity! Hide not their crime and let not their sin be blotted out in your sight, for they insulted the builders to their face!" (Nehemiah 3:36-37)

The opposition grew to the point of physical attacks on the workers, at which point Nehemiah tells us, "From that time on, however, only half my able men took a hand in the work, while the other half, armed with spears, bucklers, bows, and breastplates, stood guard behind the whole house of Judah as they rebuilt the wall" (Nehemiah 4:10). There were plots against Nehemiah's life as well.

If you have been one of the faithful who is trying to "rebuild the temple" of our faith through fidelity to the liturgical rubrics, I'm sure you see the similarities between your own battle and the battle fought by the Jews as they rebuilt the temple at Jerusalem! Not only are we rebuilding the temple, but we are rebuilding the wall – the wall that separates our faith from the secular influences that lead away from the truths of the Faith and down the slippery slope of moral relativism, which a number of popes have warned against. Indeed, the physical rebuilding of the temple was not the only "rebuilding" that took place. Chapter 8 of Nehemiah describes how Ezra was called upon by the people to "bring forth the book of the law of Moses which the Lord prescribed for Israel" (Nehemiah 8:1). And far from complaining about a long service, the people stood and listened as Ezra read "from daybreak till midday"!

The book of Ezra also recounts that the people had not been faithful to the laws of the faith: "…they have taken some of their daughters as wives for themselves and their sons, and thus they have desecrated the holy race with the peoples of the land. Furthermore, the leaders and rulers have taken a leading part in this apostasy!" (Ezra 9:2). I think we can see parallels here with our own culture – not necessarily with regard to the specific issue of Catholics marrying outside the Church, but with the "marriage" of our Faith to the errors of our secular society. Our Catholic Faith has been desecrated by this, and indeed, even some of our shepherds have taken a part in the watering down of Catholic precepts.

The battle for the rebuilding of Jerusalem was long and hard, and fraught with peril, but the people did not lose hope. Nor should we! The Israelites persevered in their mission and task, and so should we. It can be daunting to face the criticisms and sometimes even calumny of one's fellow parishioners, but it is important that each one of us continue to respectfully request correction of liturgical abuse. We have documents to support our endeavor, just as the Jewish people had the document of a former monarch to justify their rebuilding of the temple at Jerusalem – for instance, there is the instruction *Redeptionis Sacramentum* (*On certain matters to be observed or to be avoided regarding the Most Holy* Eucharist). And we must also insist on the proper implementation of the changes mandated by Vatican II – and point out the changes that have occurred that were *not* mandated and have perhaps been harmful to the Church.

It is true that we may not witness the changes we'd like to see in our own life times, but we should find hope in noting that progress *is* being made. For instance, though many "traditionalist" types feared that Pope Francis would turn his back on the EF Mass, that fear seems unfounded at this point. The Holy Father recently declined to heed the advice of a group of bishops who wanted to squelch the traditional Latin Mass. One translation says:

> "Then it was the turn of the bishop of Conversano and Monopoli, Domenico Padovano, who recounted to the clergy of his diocese how the priority of the bishops of the region of Tavoliere had been that of explaining to the Pope that the Mass in the old rite was creating great divisions within the Church. The underlying message: *Summorum Pontificum* should be cancelled, or at least strongly limited. But Francis said no."[62]

We have the favor of the Holy Father, and so must press on with the rebuilding. There is reason for hope!

In addition, there are bishops and archbishops here and there who are standing the ground for the EF Mass, who clearly see the benefits of tradition and good liturgy. For instance the Archbishop of Ferrara-Comacchio, His Excellency Most Reverend. Luigi Negri, offered the following comments in a Pentecost Sunday homily (my **emphases**):

> Benedict XVI showed his pastoral mercy by allowing this for individual Catholics or small groups who need not have a precise legal size. These are the "small groups" of the faithful who have **the right and the duty** to be able to come to this Mass.

> Now you have it all in your hands, and the Church allows you to spread it freely.

> There can be no one, no Diocese in Italy or anywhere in the world, who can stop you doing this. If any Bishop ever dares to say "no" to you, **he must be brought before an**

---

[62] http://wdtprs.com/blog/2013/05/pope-francis-shoots-down-bishops-who-want-summorum-pontificum-overturned/

ecclesiastical tribunal immediately. But before anything like that happens, there must be dialogue among the faithful who want the older Liturgy, and between the faithful and any priest who wants to help you take part in this beautiful Mass.

…Try this older Liturgy for yourselves! Try out the truths of your faith! Try out the truths of your charity! Give impetus to your mission! Be like those who try out the same truths with the reformed Liturgy in the truth of their Faith and charity: they are two treasures for the same people. People can be said to be **grown-up Catholics** if they understand these freedoms the Church gives them. Liturgical freedom is not something the Church merely gives: She guarantees it!

…I am one of the few bishops (I am afraid to say we are very few) to have gained from all this a **deeper sense of our identity in our dealings with God.** It is truly a great thing; and not just for those who practice it, but **for the whole Church.**

Let me sum up by saying that this is why you must try to get as many people as possible to walk down this path of yours.[63]

Closer to home (especially to me personally!) is a US prelate who gives us hope: Archbishop Alexander Sample of the Archdiocese of Portland, Oregon. In October of 2012, when he was still the bishop of the Diocese of Marquette, Michigan, I considered him a breath of fresh air among our bishops. Then-Bishop Sample had written an article for the Diocesan newspaper entitled "A Liturgical Quiz and An Invitation"[64] which said in part:

---

[63] http://wdtprs.com/blog/2013/05/archbishop-on-the-tlm-you-must-try-to-get-as-many-people-as-possible-to-walk-down-this-path-of-yours/
[64]http://www.upcatholic.org/WebProject.asp?CodeId=7.6.6.4&BookCode=2012050
4&SectionIndex=0&PageIndex=2

I propose a brief quiz on the Sacred Liturgy. Answer true or false to the following statements: 1) Vatican II changed the language of the Mass from Latin to the vernacular (in our case, English). 2) Vatican II replaced the signing of Gregorian chant at Mass with more contemporary vernacular music.

If you answered "true" to one or both of these statements, you should hear a buzzer going off right now indicating at least one incorrect answer. I am sure that this will come as a surprise to many…

He then quoted relevant paragraphs from *Sacrosanctum Concilium* as evidence that Latin and Gregorian chant were never diminished in value, and that "these guiding statements from Vatican II have not been fully adhered to, and have sometimes simply been ignored." He added:

Just on the issue of singing Gregorian chant at Mass, far from enjoying a "pride of place" in the liturgy, when was the last time you heard it sung or sang it yourself at Mass? Surely "pride of place" means more than an occasional sung *Sanctus* or *Agnus Dei.*

After assuring his readers that he is not proposing a "simple return to all Latin and Gregorian chant in the Mass", he noted:

What I am saying is that, in our ongoing efforts to renew and reform the Sacred Liturgy, we need to go back to the sources that gave us the direction for liturgical renewal, especially the actual Vatican II document on the Liturgy…[W]e need to interpret the liturgical reforms called for by Vatican II in light of the whole liturgical tradition of the Church, as an organic development, and not a break with the past.

This especially applies to the area of music in the Sacred Liturgy. Let's face it, in most places liturgical music has become simply selecting the four hymns for Mass (entrance, offertory, communion, and recessional). Many might be surprised to learn that this is not at all our liturgical tradition and is not what was envisioned by Vatican II. But that is what we have become used to.

The Church's tradition actually calls for us to "sing the Mass," not sing "at" Mass. The texts of the Mass given in the Missal are meant to be sung. Instead we often just paste on the four hymns which may or may not related to the actual texts of the Mass. Not sure what this means? Read on!

As bishop of Marquette, this prelate also issued a wonderful pastoral letter on sacred music called "Rejoice in the Lord Always"[65]. If he can implement something similar in the Archdiocese of Portland, a major victory will be won! In the meantime, judging by his words and actions in his previous diocese, Archbishop Sample's appointment to Portland, in and of itself, is beacon of hope – not just a glimmer!

And so it goes. There are good and holy shepherds out there… perhaps not as many as we would hope to find, and perhaps the good ones always seem to be "somewhere else" rather than in our own backyard. Still, it should give us joy to see advances being made in *any* diocese or parish regarding the restoration of a reverent liturgy – whether in the old form or the new. We've been promised that the gates of Hell will not prevail against our Church, and that is the hope we must cling to!

In the meantime, whenever you go to a deficient Mass, imagine what Our Lord suffers as He endures the same thing, and pray this prayer:

---

[65] http://www.dioceseofmarquette.org/UserFiles/Bishop/PastoralLetter-RejoiceInTheLordAlways.pdf

O Most Holy Trinity, Father, Son, and Holy Ghost,
I offer to You the most Precious Body and Blood,
Soul and Divinity of Jesus Christ,
present in all the tabernacles of the world,
in reparation for the sacrileges, outrages, and indifference
by which He Himself is offended.
And through the infinite merits of His most Sacred Heart
and the Immaculate Heart of Mary,
I beg of you the conversion of poor sinners.

Appendices

Appendix A

The response from the CDW was in the form of a letter (Protocol No. 930/08/L), dated November 22, 2008, signed by Father Anthony Ward, SM, Under-secretary of the Congregation. It was addressed to two men who had written requesting clarification about the matter of blessings, and a photocopy may be viewed at http://forums.catholic.com/attachment.php?s=ec9e98e59e53574626e d2df5aedff471&attachmentid=4690&d=1228783198.

See further commentary on the letter at http://www.ewtn.com/library/liturgy/zlitur263.htm

The main text of the letter is as follows:

> Dear Mr. XXX and Mr. XXX:
>
> This Congregation for Divine Worship and the Discipline of the Sacraments acknowledges receipt of your kind letter of 13 August, 2008 and would like to thank you for your interest and suggestions. This matter is presently under the attentive study of the Congregation.
>
> > For the present, therefore, this Dicastery wishes to limit itself to the following observations:
>
> 1. The liturgical blessing of the Holy Mass is properly given to each and to all at the conclusion of the Mass, just a few moments subsequent to the distribution of Holy Communion.
>
> 2. Lay people, within the context of Holy Mass, are unable to confer blessings. These blessings, rather, are the competence of the priest (cf. *Ecclesia de Mysterio*, *Notitiae* 34 (15 Aug. 1997), art. 6, § 2; Canon 1169, § 2; and Roman *Ritual De Benedictionibus* (1985), n. 18).

3. Furthermore, the laying on of a hand or hands – which has its own sacramental significance, inappropriate here – by those distributing Holy Communion, in substitution for its reception, is to be explicitly discouraged.

4. The Apostolic Exhortation *Familiaris Consortio* n. 84, "forbids any pastor, for whatever reason or pretext even of a pastoral nature, to perform ceremonies of any kind for divorced people who remarry". To be feared is that any form of blessing in substitution for communion would give the impression that the divorced and remarried have been returned, in some sense, to the status of Catholics in good standing.

5. In a similar way, for others who are not to be admitted to Holy Communion in accord with the norm of law, the Church's discipline has already made clear that they should not approach Holy Communion nor receive a blessing. This would include non-Catholics and those envisaged in can. 915 (i.e., those under the penalty of excommunication or interdict, and others who obstinately persist in manifest grave sin).

Please continue to pray for the Church's minsters that they ever become more worthy of the mystery they celebrate.

Appendix B

This document is available in various places on the web; I found it at: http://www.adoremus.org/concerts.html

** ** ** ** **

Concerts in Churches

Protocol number 1251/87

November 5, 1987

(The following declaration of the Congregation for Divine Worship and the Discipline of the Sacraments was sent to the presidents of the national conferences of bishops and through them to commissions on Liturgy and sacred art.)

I. MUSIC IN CHURCHES OTHER THAN DURING LITURGICAL CELEBRATIONS

1. The interest shown in music is one of the marks of contemporary culture. The ease with which it is possible to listen at home to classical works, by means of radio, records, cassettes and television, has in no way diminished the pleasure of attending live concerts, but on the contrary has actually enhanced it. This is encouraging, because music and song contribute to elevating the human spirit.

The increase in the number of concerts in general has in some countries given rise to a more frequent use of churches for such events. Various reasons are given for this: local needs, where for example it is not easy to find suitable places; acoustical considerations, for which churches are often ideal; aesthetic reasons of fittingness, that is to present the works in the setting for which they were originally written; purely practical reasons, for example facilities for organ recitals: in a word churches are considered to be in many ways apt places for holding a concert.

2. Alongside this contemporary development a new situation has arisen in the Church.

The Scholae cantorum have not had frequent occasion to execute their traditional repertory of sacred polyphonic music within the context of a liturgical celebration.

For this reason, the initiative has been taken to perform this sacred music in church in the form of a concert. The same has happened with Gregorian chant, which has come to form part of concert programs both inside and outside the church.

Another important factor emerges from the so-called "spiritual concerts," so-termed because the music performed in them can be considered as religious, because of the theme chosen, or on account of the nature of the texts set to music, or because of the venue for the performance.

Such events are in some cases accompanied by readings, prayers and moments of silence. Given such features they can almost be compared to a "devotional exercise."

3. The increased numbers of concerts held in churches has given rise to doubts in the minds of pastors and rectors of churches as to the extent to which such events are really necessary.

A general opening of churches for concerts could give rise to complaints by a number of the faithful, yet on the other hand an outright refusal could lead to some misunderstanding.

Firstly, it is necessary to consider the significance and purpose of a Christian church. For this, the Congregation for Divine Worship considers it opportune to propose to the episcopal conferences, and in so far as it concerns them, to the national commissions of Liturgy and music, some observations and interpretations for the canonical norms concerning the use of churches for various kinds of music: music and song, music of religious inspiration and music of non-religious character.

4. At this juncture it is necessary to re-read recent documents which treat of the subject, in particular the Constitution on the Liturgy *Sacrosanctum Concilium*, the instruction *Musicam Sacram* of March 5, 1967, the instruction *Liturgicae Instaurationes* of September 5, 1970, in addition to the prescription of the code of Canon Law, can. 1210, 1213 and 1222.

In this present letter the primary concern is with musical performances outside of the celebration of the Liturgy.

II. POINTS FOR CONSIDERATION

The character and purpose of churches

5. According to tradition as expressed in the rite for the dedication of a church and altar, churches are primarily places where the people of God gather, and are "made one as the Father, the Son and the Holy Spirit are one, and are the Church, the temple of God built with living stones, in which the Father is worshipped in spirit and in truth." Rightly so, from ancient times the name "church" has been extended to the building in which the Christian community unite to hear the word of God, to pray together, to receive the sacraments, to celebrate the Eucharist and to prolong its celebration in the adoration of the Blessed Sacrament (Cf. Order of the Dedication of a Church, ch. II, 1).

Churches, however, cannot be considered simply as public places for any kind of meeting. They are sacred places, that is, "set apart" in a permanent way for divine worship by their dedication and blessing.

As visible constructions, churches are signs of the pilgrim Church on earth; they are images that proclaim the heavenly Jerusalem, places in which are actualized the mystery of the communion between man and God. Both in urban areas and in the countryside, the church remains the house of God, and the sign of his dwelling among men. It remains a sacred place, even when no liturgical celebration is taking place.

In a society disturbed by noise, especially in big cities, churches are also an oasis where men gather, in silence and in prayer, to seek peace of soul and the light of faith.

That will only be possible in so far as churches maintain their specific identity. When churches are used for ends other than those for which they were built, their role as a sign of the Christian mystery is put at risk, with more or less serious harm to the teaching of the faith and to the sensitivity of the People of God, according to the Lord's words: "My house is a house of prayer" (Lk 19:46).

Importance of sacred music

6. Sacred music, whether vocal or instrumental, is of importance. Music is sacred "in so far as it is composed for the celebration of divine worship and possesses integrity of form" (*Musicam sacram* n. 4a). The church considers it a "treasure of inestimable value, greater even than that of any other art," recognizing that it has a "ministerial function in the service of the Lord" (Cf. SC n. 112); and recommending that it be "preserved and fostered with great care" (SC n. 114).

Any performance of sacred music which takes place during a celebration, should be fully in harmony with that celebration. This often means that musical compositions which date from a period when the active participation of the faithful was not emphasized as the source of the authentic Christian spirit (SC n. 14; Pius X *Tra le sollecitudini*) are no longer to be considered suitable for inclusion within liturgical celebrations.

Analogous changes of perception and awareness have occurred in other areas involving the artistic aspect of divine worship: for example, the sanctuary has been restructured, with the president's chair, the ambo and the altar versus populum. Such changes have not been made in a spirit of disregard for the past, but have been deemed necessary in the pursuit of an end of greater importance, namely the active participation of the faithful. The limitation which such changes impose on certain musical works can be overcome by arranging for their performance outside the context of liturgical celebration in a concert of sacred music.

Organ

7. The performance of purely instrumental pieces on the organ during liturgical celebrations today is limited. In the past the organ took the place of the active participation of the faithful, and reduced the people to the role of "silent and inert spectators" of the celebration (Pius XI, *Divini cultus*, n. 9).

It is legitimate for the organ to accompany and sustain the singing either of the assembly or the choir within the celebration. On the other hand, the organ must never be used to accompany the prayers or chants of the celebrant nor the readings proclaimed by the reader or the deacon.

In accordance with tradition, the organ should remain silent during penitential seasons (Lent and Holy Week), during Advent and Liturgy for the dead. When, however, there is real pastoral need, the organ can be used to support the singing.

It is fitting that the organ be played before and after a celebration as a preparation and conclusion of the celebration. It is of considerable importance that in all churches, and especially those of some importance, there should be trained musicians and instruments of good quality. Care should be given to the maintenance of organs and respect shown towards their historical character both in form and tone.

III. PRACTICAL DIRECTIVES

8. The regulation of the use of churches is stipulated by canon 1210 of the Code of Canon Law:

"In a sacred place only those things are to be permitted which serve to exercise or promote worship, piety and religion. Anything out of harmony with the holiness the place is forbidden. The Ordinary may, however, for individual cases, permit other uses, provided they are not contrary to the sacred character of the place."

The principle that the use of the church must not offend the sacredness of the place determines the criteria by which the doors of a church may be opened to a concert of sacred or religious music, as also the concomitant exclusion of every other type of music. The most beautiful symphonic music, for example, is not in itself of religious character. The definition of sacred or religious music depends explicitly on the original intended use of the musical pieces or songs, and likewise on their content. It is not legitimate to provide for the execution in the church of music which is not of religious inspiration and which was composed with a view to performance in a certain precise secular context, irrespective of whether the music would be judged classical or contemporary, of high quality or of a popular nature. On the one hand, such performances would not respect the sacred character of the church, and on the other, would result in the music being performed in an unfitting context.

It pertains to the ecclesiastical authority to exercise without constraint its governance of sacred places (Cf. canon 1213), and hence to regulate the use of churches in such a way as to safeguard their sacred character.

9. Sacred music, that is to say music which was composed for the Liturgy, but which for various reasons can no longer be performed during a liturgical celebration, and religious music, that is to say music inspired by the text of sacred scripture or the Liturgy and which has reference to God, the Blessed Virgin Mary, to the saints or to the Church, may both find a place in the church building, but outside liturgical celebration. The playing of the organ or other musical performance, whether vocal or instrumental, may: "serve to promote piety or religion." In particular they may:

a. prepare for the major liturgical feasts, or lend to these a more festive character beyond the moment of actual celebration;

b. bring out the particular character of the different liturgical seasons;

c. create in churches a setting of beauty conducive to meditation, so as to arouse even in those who are distant from the Church an openness to spiritual values;

d. create a context which favors and makes accessible the proclamation of God's word, as for example, a sustained reading of the Gospel;

e. keep alive the treasures of Church music which must not be lost; musical pieces and songs composed for the Liturgy but which cannot in any way be conveniently incorporated into liturgical celebrations in modern times; spiritual music, such as oratorios and religious cantatas which can still serve as vehicles for spiritual communication;

f. assist visitors and tourists to grasp more fully the sacred character of a church, by means of organ concerts at prearranged times.

10. When the proposal is made that there should be a concert in a church, the Ordinary is to grant the permission per modum actus. These concerts should be occasional events. This excludes permission for a series of concerts, for example in the case of a festival or a cycle of concerts.

When the Ordinary considers it to be necessary, he can, in the conditions foreseen in the Code of Canon Law (can. 1222, para. 2) designate a church that is no longer used for divine service, to be an "auditorium" for the performance of sacred or religious music, and also of music not specifically religious but in keeping with the character of the place.

In this task the bishop should be assisted by the diocesan commission for Liturgy and sacred music.

In order that the sacred character of a church be conserved in the matter of concerts, the Ordinary can specify that:

a. Requests are to be made in writing, in good time, indicating the date and time of the proposed concert, the program, giving the works and the names of the composers.

b. After having received the authorization of the Ordinary, the rectors and parish priests of the churches should arranged details with the choir and orchestra so that the requisite norms are observed.

c. Entrance to the church must be without payment and open to all.

d. The performers and the audience must be dressed in a manner which is fitting to the sacred character of the place.

e. The musicians and the singers should not be placed in the sanctuary. The greatest respect is to be shown to the altar, the president's chair and the ambo.

f. The Blessed Sacrament should be, as far as possible, reserved in a side chapel or in another safe and suitably adorned place (Cf. C.I.C., can 928, par. 4).

g. The concert should be presented or introduced not only with historical or technical details, but also in a way that fosters a deeper understanding and an interior participation on the part of the listeners.

h. The organizer of the concert will declare in writing that he accepts legal responsibilities for expenses involved, for leaving the church in order and for any possible damage incurred.

11. The above practical directives should be of assistance to the bishops and rectors of churches in their pastoral responsibility to maintain the sacred character of their churches, designed for sacred celebrations, prayer and silence.

Such indications should not be interpreted as a lack of interest in the art of music.

The treasury of sacred music is a witness to the way in which the Christian faith promotes culture.

By underlining the true value of sacred or religious music, Christian musicians and members of scholae cantorum should feel that they are being encouraged to continue this tradition and to keep it alive for the service of the faith, as expressed by the Second Vatican Council in its message to artists:

"Do not hesitate to put your talent at the service of the Divine Truth. The world in which we live has need of beauty in order not to lose hope. Beauty, like truth, fills the heart with joy. And this, thanks to your hands" (Cf. Second Vatican Council, Message to Artists, December 8, 1965).

Rome, November 5, 1987
Paul Augustine Card. Mayer, O.S.B.
Prefect

Virgilio Noë
Tit. Archbishop of Voncaria
Secretary

****

The text appeared in *Sacred Music,* Vol. 114, N. 4 (Winter) 1987

Made in the USA
Lexington, KY
02 October 2018